How to Build a
FLATIRON SKIFF

Simple Steps Using Basic Tools

K. D. Jones

Photos by K. D. Jones and Mark Freeland

Drawings by K. D. Jones and Marc Shoemaker

Schiffer Publishing Ltd®

4880 Lower Valley Road • Atglen, PA 19310

Dedication

For my dad, Keith D. Jones, 1920–2013, who taught me that patience is the best tool you can have, and to all who took the time over the years to teach me a thing or two about traditional woodworking.

The photos in this book were taken at the Indiana State Museum; the Central Canal in downtown Indianapolis, Indiana; the Johnson County Historical Museum, Franklin, Indiana; Camp Atterbury, Edinburgh, Indiana; and my boat shop in Virginia near the Potomac River. For inspiration I used the boats I remembered as a child, Thoreau's boat, *Musketaquid*, and local skiffs of the Chesapeake Bay area.

Copyright © 2015 by K. D. Jones
Library of Congress Control Number: 2015942148

Cover designed by Justin Watkinson
Interior designed by Matt Goodman
Type set in Brigthon & Minion

ISBN: 978-0-7643-4885-3
Printed in China

Published by Schiffer Publishing, Ltd.
4880 Lower Valley Road
Atglen, PA 19310
Phone: (610) 593-1777; Fax: (610) 593-2002
E-mail: Info@schifferbooks.com

For our complete selection of fine books on this and related subjects, please visit our website at www.schifferbooks.com. You may also write for a free catalog.

This book may be purchased from the publisher. Please try your bookstore first.

We are always looking for people to write books on new and related subjects. If you have an idea for a book, please contact us at proposals@schifferbooks.com.

Schiffer Publishing's titles are available at special discounts for bulk purchases for sales promotions or premiums. Special editions, including personalized covers, corporate imprints, and excerpts can be created in large quantities for special needs. For more information, contact the publisher.

Contents

Introduction: Simple, Functional, Elegant

This book is about how to build a good boat. It is an eclectic story with a glimpse into the past, and a textbook of instructions, photographs, and drawings. It is also about my boat-building journey and my preference for common materials, wood purchased from DIY home stores, and simple hand tools as a quiet alternative to power equipment. And it's about dreaming a little, pushing your imagination, enjoying your boat, and creating your own skiff stories.

The boats in this book represent a technique almost lost to modern culture—building by hand and eye. The flatiron skiff can be constructed simply and at a reasonable cost. The basic skiff design reached most of its development in the late nineteenth century, so this is not your typical wood-and-epoxy construction. There are hundreds of variations of these still-popular boats.

When I first started building boats, wooden boat building had mostly dried up; everything was being made from fiberglass. When I searched the public library and new and used bookstores, everything I could find included complicated drawings and terms I couldn't understand. Most of the boats in these books were yachts and commercial craft, and far out of my price range. I found a few magazine articles about boat-building with plywood, but there was little information on the simple boats I remembered as a child.

Much later, wooden boat-making made a comeback, starting on the coasts and spreading to anywhere there was water. New books were published, but I still could not find information on the boats I remembered, and much of the information was not basic enough for first-time builders.

I collected all of my resource material, including the simple designs I had encountered along the way. The designs that fascinate me the most are flatiron skiffs, which are solidly built from local materials, and practical, too. During this time I was inspired while reading one of Henry David Thoreau's journals. In 1839, Thoreau and his brother, John, built a boat and went on a camping trip down the Concord and Merrimack Rivers. Thoreau writes:

> Our boat, which had cost us a week's labor in the spring, was in form like a fisherman's dory, fifteen feet long by three and a half in breadth at the widest part, painted green below, with a border of blue, with reference to the two elements in which it was to spend its existence. It had been loaded the evening before at our door, half a mile from the river, with potatoes and melons from a patch which we had cultivated, and a few utensils, and was provided with wheels in order to be rolled around falls, as well as with two sets of oars, and several slender poles for shoving in shallow places, and also two masts, one of which served for a tent-pole at night; for a buffalo skin was to be our bed, and a tent of cotton cloth our roof. It was strongly built but heavy, and hardly of better model than usual. If rightly made, a boat would be a sort of amphibious animal, a creature of two elements, related by one half its structure to some swift and shapely fish, and by the other to some strong-winged and graceful bird. The fish shows where there should be the greatest breadth of beam and depth in the hold; its fins direct where to set the oars, and the tail gives some hint for the form and position of the rudder. The bird shows how to rig and trim the sails, and what form to give the prow that it may balance the boat and divide the air and water best. These hints we had but partially obeyed. But the eyes, though they are no sailors, will never be satisfied with any model, however fashionable, which does not answer all of the requisitions of art. However, as art is all of a ship but the wood, and yet

the wood alone will rudely serve the purpose of a ship, so our boat being of wood gladly availed itself of the old law that the heavier shall float the lighter, and though a dull water fowl, proved sufficient for our purpose.

After more research on nineteenth-century boat building, I decided to try what I now call my Thoreau approach. The skiffs we are going to build follow this theme. These boats are flat-bottomed and made from wood. They can be rowed, powered with a small outboard motor, or configured for a sail. About 12–16 feet long, they can be built by a beginner using a few hand tools and materials from the local home lumber store.

I consider this type of boat building an art, and what sets it apart is its simplicity. When I build a boat this way the project becomes personal. I have an idea, a picture in my head, but I don't know what the boat will look like in its final form. I let a lot of things happen and deal with surprises along the way. Surprises are fun, challenging, and good for the creative spirit.

Being resourceful was a way of life long ago, and it is useful today, too. I try to limit myself to a few materials and tools. I like to think of this method as practical. This is the way I learned to build boats.

With the revival of wooden boat building there are now many building methods for amateur and professional builders to choose from. Some methods use epoxy and fiberglass cloth, carbon fiber, marine plywood, and even metals. These methods are good, but they can be costly and overly complicated for the first-timer. For that reason, we will build our skiff using construction techniques from a time when folks used local materials and ingenuity. Although I am no longer a novice, I still prefer this way of building because it is quick, easy, and affordable.

Growing up on the West Fork of the White River in Indiana, I learned to row in a beast of a thing my uncles had built using scrap lumber from an old barn. The oars did not match, but in spite of it all my cousins and I had a great time playing on the river. Just about everyone we knew had a flat-bottomed boat. With a few weekends of work, you could fashion a boat and be on the river by summer. Some boats looked and performed better than others, but getting out on the water was the most important thing. As kids, we knew our boats would get muddy, filled with sand, loaded with bait cans and fishing poles. We didn't have time for polishing brass and varnishing teak, and none of us had ever seen a boat with that stuff anyway.

In this book we'll travel back in time for guidance on how things used to be done. We will get some wood from our local lumber store, a few other supplies, and add imagination. Our boat will have sweet lines; when finished, it will be simple, functional, and elegant.

1

Getting Started

Getting started is often the hardest part. Think of planning your project in your head as the beginning, and you will have started your boat. I find it fun to discover how these boats were used, and how their use affected their designs. After years of messing around with other boats, I mostly build small skiffs now. These are usually less than 16 feet long, a handy size. You don't need much space for building. Build it outside if you wish.

All projects are best tackled by separating them into smaller parts. After each small part is completed, move along to the next one, and before you know it, you are launching your boat. Before we start buying materials, cutting boards, and fastening parts together, let's talk about boat-building history and the tools we will use.

Small Skiffs

The word skiff comes from the German language and simply means a small boat. The flatiron skiff is shaped similar to the old household pressing irons that were heated on top of a stove. With their pointed bow and flat stern, the design is easily recognizable. Not all skiffs are flat bottomed. Many of the traditional flatiron skiffs were often boxy looking; however, they can be given a graceful look, too. We can accomplish this by adding curves here and there to soften hard edges and improve the overall appearance. If you add color, a waterline stripe, or a piece of trim, the graceful appearance is enhanced.

All boats were once working craft, as there was little recreational time for the average person. They were designed to stand up to the everyday rigors of fishing, harbor transportation, and cargo carrying. That doesn't mean folks didn't take their working boats out for an afternoon of fun on water. As leisure time increased, enterprising owners cleaned up and rented out their boats for Sunday afternoon excursions.

A century ago, two men working together were expected to build a skiff in a few days, and painting was optional. Made from local woods and iron nails, these tough boats were used until they fell apart. The old boats were cut up and put into the wood stove to heat the shop, and replacements were made. Parts like row locks, cleats, and bow eyes might be salvaged for use on another boat.

The average wage for a skilled shipwright in the late nineteenth century was about a dollar a day. Most work days were ten or more hours, six days a week. There were no unions, no benefits, no paid sick days or leave, and no one had automobiles. Most lived as close as they could to their jobs, and seldom could workers earn enough money to purchase the boats they built.

During this period, most boat yards had power tools such as big ship saws, thickness planers, lathes, and drill presses. These were usually powered by a steam engine running a common shaft arrangement where leather belts would transfer the energy to the individual machines. In later years, electric motors replaced steam engines to power the shop. Large power tools were used to process and shape the rough boards from the lumber mill into usable planks. Just about everything else was accomplished with hand tools.

Most skilled tradesmen collected their tools over time and from many sources. It was common for each boat builder to have one large chest for storage and another small tote to carry out to the boat he was working on. I use a similar method. Depending on what I am doing on a given day, I will lift out specialized compartments to take to the job. For example, planes and chisels are in one box, rasps and files are in another, and so on. I also keep an assortment of common household tools in a box made from scrap lumber with a rope handle.

A Straightforward Process

Why build a boat rather than purchase one? For one thing, building this type of skiff doesn't cost much if you use some of the older methods. With this straightforward process, you will also gain new abilities and confidence in yourself as a woodworker. Do it because you want a challenge and because it is fun. It is rewarding to make something you can use with family and friends. These simple boats will get you out on the water with minimal effort and cost.

In my boat building classes, we don't use formal plans, and that puts almost everyone on the same page. In the past, small boats were usually made from a design sketched on a piece of paper or a little model carved with a jack knife. In the trade this is called building by eye. As the old boat builders would say, "If she's eye sweet, she'll sail sweet."

I suggest you read through this book twice—once for an overview and the second time for clarity. Let it inspire your imagination. Study the photographs and make notes if you wish. During the second read you can decide what type of variation you want to build. This allows you to get organized, shop for materials, locate a suitable space, and make your budget. The good news is that you don't need to purchase all of your materials up front. You can buy them when you need them at your local lumber store. If you wish to purchase marine hardware or other marine items, reference the list of suppliers in the appendix.

Halfway through this project, you might decide that building your own boat isn't your cup of tea. That is perfectly fine. I have seen many people invest a lot of time and money on a project that was becoming a burden and probably wouldn't get completed. The good thing about these skiffs is they can be built for around $500. I have been able to keep my costs stable over the years by using common building materials, standard fasteners, and eliminating waste. Each year I get a little better at saving money on materials. I will cover these details in subsequent chapters.

If you decide to try your hand at boat building, you will soon discover that it has a language all its own, like any other technology. I have tried to use as little jargon as possible, and to explain the terms I do use. Learning the maritime language is part of the fun.

When the Boating World Changed

In the second half of the twentieth century, a shorter work week became standard, and leisure activities such as boating expanded to fill that time. During this period, a new material that originated in the technology of World War II changed boat building forever. Resin-impregnated glass cloth, or fiberglass, could be molded into thousands of complex shapes, and boats could be mass-produced affordably. This new material could have permanent color molded in, did not rot, and needed little care compared to wood. Best of all these new boats didn't leak and the seasonal caulking and painting once required to seal the wood hulls was eliminated. Boat companies converted to this new material almost overnight.

The renewed interest in wooden boats comes from several factors. Wood is pretty. A fiberglass boat doesn't draw the attention a gleaming wood runabout does when it pulls up to the dock. When you travel to the big wooden boat shows, like the ones at Lake Tahoe or in Clayton, New York, you will get to see a few of the last Gold Cuppers, all varnished mahogany and driven by powerful engines right out of the jazz age. Even my little skiff gets attention and compliments when I sail into a marina. When I tell folks I built it myself for a fraction of the cost of a comparable fiberglass boat, they are intrigued.

Wood is still a wonderful material. It is much easier for the amateur builder to create in wood than any other material. Wood does not require a production mold. Other than shavings and sawdust, traditional wood construction isn't messy, and harsh toxic chemicals aren't needed, either.

Traditional and Modern

When I was a child learning my way around the river, everyone I knew had a variation of these flat bottomed boats tied up to their docks or to a tree on shore. Some had little putt-putt inboard motors, a few had outboard motors, and most had oars. It was not uncommon then to still see watermen checking their trout lines, bottle jigs or traps.

In 1945, when my uncle Lowell O'Brien returned from the war in the Pacific, he went to work in the family music store. Shortly after his return he heard that a city park on the White River near his home was looking for some new rowboats. Over the weekend, he and his brother Harry built their first skiff in the back of the store, launched it at the town bridge, and rowed it to the park the following Monday. They didn't have time to paint it and some of the seams had not swollen tight enough to make it leak-proof, but the park service liked the little boat and ordered ten more just like it. Then the brothers had to figure out how they were going to build and deliver their order.

We lived across the street from the music store. I had just been born and my father was looking for extra work to pay the bills. He was enlisted as a helper until the newly formed company got on its feet. As their popularity increased, these boats were sold all over the state. The basic design didn't change much. Lowell called them "two plankers," because they were made from two planks of white pine for each side and cross-planked with cedar on the bottom.

When I was about ten years old, I helped out in the O'Brien boat shop along with my cousins. At first I wasn't allowed to do much except watch, but later I was promoted to sweeping, painting, and then lending a hand with the building. These designs were all originally built of local wood, without plans, to a simple length-to-breadth ratio of three or four times longer than wide, and with a maximum hull depth of two feet. Most of these boats were nailed together without glue and the seams were coated with white lead, caulked with cotton, primed with thinned exterior oil-based house paint, and then finished with another coat of the same paint. Often the bottoms were painted with thick black paint or tar. You can still build a boat this way, but some of the materials used back then are not available now.

For me, there is no set definition of the American version of a flatiron skiff, because the design itself goes back several hundred years. I do use a few modern materials for convenience, which I will cover in detail as we build our boat. For example, unless someone wants a cross-plank cedar bottom, I use marine plywood for the bottom. The older-style plank bottoms only work if the boat is left in the water, where they swell and stay tight. If the boat is to be launched for the day and returned to a trailer, the plank bottom will dry out, and the constant swelling and drying will eventually ruin it. So if you are going to keep your skiff at home and take it to the water, a plywood bottom is the way to go. However, I will cover

cedar plank bottoms, too, in chapter 3.

I also use modern corrosion-resistant fasteners because they last longer than common steel nails. Many times I use acrylic paints because they are easy to clean up. I still use oil-based paints and varnish when it is applicable to the boat design, or to the period if it is to be a replica. I don't use red or white lead anymore, even though it is still used for large wooden ships. I don't want to get lead poisoning.

Many of the boats I grew up with were never painted, and inexpensive wood was the material of choice. Nothing was wasted, either. I remember spending hours with my cousins pulling nails from old barn planks and straightening them on a piece of railroad iron, and then we would throw the nails into a bucket of used motor oil. Some of the old barn planks even found their way into the boats. I don't go to those extremes anymore, but some frugality is a good thing. I do my best not to have a lot of unused wood lying around after a boat is completed. I always have some though, and it is used for the next build or for extra benches and sawhorses. I never seem to have enough small benches, because I am always giving them away.

I prefer to use hand tools. I used to call them non-powered, but that isn't really correct, because they are all driven by my muscles and strength. A good week of boat building in this fashion will help you get in shape. When building this way, you can introduce children to wood working with little danger from spinning blades or rotating machinery. I find it challenging and fun to use my muscle powered tools limiting my exposure to loud noise, airborne dust, and the real possibility of cutting off a finger or two with a power saw.

This building method will not require a lot of exact measurements or angles, either. In most cases, measurements are rounded up to the nearest inch and angles are figured out by eye, with small adjustments with a hand plane, wood rasp, and sandpaper. Most of the dimensions will be approximate; you can use them as they are, or expand or reduce them a bit to accommodate your lumber.

No Building Jig or Lofting

Many small wood boats are built upside-down on a building jig. The jig establishes the locations of the mold stations and holds everything rigid while the boat is being planked. After the hull is completed, it is lifted from the jig and the interior seats, braces, and decks are installed. This is a good way to build boats, and most small boat plans specify this method. The process requires lofting, also referred to as lifting the boat's measurements from the plans to make full-size patterns. These patterns are then used to create accurate mold stations and installed on your building frame, the jig.

Sometimes the frame becomes a removable jig and sometimes a portion of it will stay within the finished boat. Lofting can be so confusing that at this point many would-be builders give up. I also constantly hear amateur boat-builders complain that it took them two weeks or more to make the jig and more money than they wanted to spend on materials that will get used only once. We are not going to build this way; we don't have plans to build from, anyway. We will build our skiff right-side up, as skiff builders did in times past.

The old-timers made their boats right-side-up on low benches, turning them upside-down to plank the bottom. When building right-side-up, you can see the shape of the boat develop, the twist in the planks, and the curve of the sheer. All of these things can be adjusted as you build. You adapt as you deal with surprises that always happen. For example, you will need to do this as you work with knots, splits in planks, warped boards, and bent or broken fasteners, to name just a few.

I have learned that not all wood planks bend the same, even though they came from the same tree. When you build by eye, these small differences can be accommodated by adjustments as you go. So what if your boat ends up 15 feet 3 inches or 15 feet 10 inches in length. If you are following a set of plans it can matter. If you purchase plans, please follow them to the letter. With more complex designs than the skiffs we are building, deviation from the drawings can change a boat's performance and compromise safety.

Mistakes, Fasteners, and Rot

Several years ago I was teaching a skiff-building class. We had completed planking the sides and had moved on to cutting out the seats and deck when we heard a loud bang like a gunshot. After inspection we discovered the top plank on the starboard side (right side looking forward) had broken in the middle where the wood fibers were weak. This often happens on wide pine boards. I try to inspect for these weaknesses, but you can't always tell what will happen until you bend the boards and stress them. There were a lot of long faces in the room, because the side planks had been glued and fastened into place with nails. It would be a big job to remove that plank and replace it with a new one.

I explained to the class the excessive stress on the plank was now eliminated because of the fracture. The plank did not look that bad, because the fracture was on a growth ring and protruded only about a half-inch. We decided to plane down the damaged area to the level of the rest of the plank and cover it with a trim piece, which we glued and screwed to provide more strength. We added another piece of trim to the opposite port side to provide symmetry (port being the left side looking forward). I have owned a lot of skiffs and I believe most mistakes don't affect performance one bit, and in my opinion they add character. Anyway, the difference between a professional and amateur is the professional is usually better at covering up mistakes. We all make them.

A hundred years ago these skiffs were assembled with iron nails and lots of white and red lead paste in the joints. The lead paste helped to waterproof the seams and control rot. No one considered the lead very toxic back then. The galvanizing process was also available around that time, but most of these boats were not considered worth the expense of galvanized nails. Plain iron nails were okay, because iron deteriorates at a much lower rate than steel, at least in fresh water. In salt water the corrosion is faster. In years past I can remember my Uncle Lowell sneaking in a few of those straightened oil-soaked nails that I had been pulling from used lumber when he had run out of the better ones. These boats were considered disposable, and building cheap as possible was the way to go.

A skiff built this way and used hard could be expected to last at least five years. Using modern fastenings and glue, with a good paint job and reasonable care, there is no reason you could not expect ten or more years out of these boats today, and maybe longer.

The subject of rot always comes up, too. Wood boats do rot, and some woods are prone to rot faster than others. In small boats like we are building, rot can be managed by keeping the boat clean. Debris that builds up in corners and under seats attracts moisture and this moisture is slow to dry out. If rot spores are present, and they usually are, it will begin in these regions. Dampness in areas where sunlight can't reach is a good breeding ground for rot, too. One of the easiest things you can do is periodic cleaning of your skiff with a mild solution of bleach, soap, and a good dose of sunlight. Never put your boat away for the winter without cleaning it. Store it upside down where air can circulate through the hull. If you can't store it inside, store it on your building benches off the ground, and cover it with a tarp. Remember to let everything breathe. In the spring, give it a good wash, inspection, and paint touch-up here and there, and you'll be ready for launching.

Epoxy and Fiberglass

At this point I am often asked about using epoxy and fiberglass cloth to encapsulate the wood and prevent rot and add additional strength. The answer is complicated. In general, the boats we are going to build are old designs and the materials we have today were unheard of back then, so in adding epoxy and fiberglass to a nineteenth-century style of plank boat does not always work very well. The planks need to move and not all epoxy is flexible, so it eventually fractures and water gets into the wood and can't get out. The wood then saturates with water, and with the summer warmth rot begins and damage is done to the once good planks.

Here is an example: A friend of mine built a plank dory and covered the outside and inside with fiberglass cloth and epoxy resin. He spent a lot of money on good materials, including the coatings, and he did a credible job glassing the boat. All went along pretty well until he noticed swelling near the transom. By the end of that summer moisture had worked its way into the planks through tiny cracks in the resin and glass, and rot began to destroy the wood cells. The epoxy also blocked the escape of the water vapor. A few years later we burned the boat on the sailing club bonfire. It could not be saved without a lot of work and expense. The dory wasn't very old.

Traditional plank boats must be allowed to expand and contract. Leaking is controlled with good, tight joints and properly caulked seams and paint. As the boats age, the old caulking needs to be removed and new caulking added with a proper paint job. When fiberglass boats came on the scene, everyone thought there would be no more boat maintenance. In a few years the fiberglass boats faded in the sunlight, and water intrusion caused damage as well as blistering. If not mixed correctly, the resins failed, and then separation of the glass layers occurred. If the fiberglass boat was built with internal wood structural members, and some of it poor quality wood at that, these often rotted and failed once moisture reached them; these problems needed repairing. In time the truth came out; all boats need some maintenance, including fiberglass, even if it is just a good periodic inspection, cleaning, and waxing.

My primary concern with some of the modern adhesives is the toxicity levels with many of the catalyzed products, mainly what most call epoxies. Epoxies have come a long way since they were first developed, but they are still toxic and must be used with safety precautions following the manufacturer's recommendations and instructions. You can find relatively safe epoxies, but they are more expensive. Epoxy is expensive anyway, so most builders want to control cost and they choose the less expensive product. Less expensive hardeners are the most likely to be more toxic. Many of the solvents used with them are also toxic and must be used with caution. Years ago I would wash up with these solvents removing glue and paint that was on my hands and not thinking about the adverse affects of the chemicals penetrating my skin and getting into my bloodstream, let alone messing with my organs. I can remember coming home from work and having difficulty breathing from the fumes as the epoxy off-gassed or solvents evaporated. Just thinking about those fumes getting into my lungs still bothers me.

With the resurgence of wood boat building has also come new technologies. These technologies have allowed the professional and amateur builder the opportunity to build designs that were previously unattainable to the traditional builder. I respect these advancements and recognize them; however, I choose not to use most of them. This is a personal choice; after working with epoxy for years I am now allergic to these resins. Unless I suit up with protective gear I am probably looking forward to a trip to the emergency room and a week-long rash with uncontrollable itching. If you choose to use these products, please be careful.

Tools of the Trade

I once saw a magazine photo in which a fishing village was building a 40-foot boat on a beach somewhere in the Caribbean. The boat had nice lines and was half finished. There was another photo of the workers' tool box, a reclaimed melon crate, and in it was a hammer, an old saw, a well-worn jack plane, and a 1-inch bolt made into a chisel. They had a hacksaw for cutting their scrap rebar into huge nails for fastening the planks. They bored their holes for the big rebar nails with a T-bar welded to a 2-foot auger. The fasteners were dipped into a tub of grease before being hammered into place. Later the bottom seams would be caulked with old bed sheets and cotton waste, and the planks swabbed with hot roof tar. The boat was being built with urgency. Payment would come when fish could be caught and sold in the market.

I have seen workers in Laos, on a tributary of the Mekong River, cutting 40-foot hardwood planks using a two-man saw with the log marked with a chalk line made with ground charcoal and old engine oil. Once the planks were cut and shaped, a long, narrow flat-bottom boat would be hammered together with handmade nails cut with a hacksaw from a thick sheet of bronze. The boat would be coated with a mix of diesel fuel, Tung oil, and other things. Later the boat might be powered with a truck engine mounted on the stern with a long shaft, or long balanced oars, and maybe a combination of both.

As you can see, it doesn't take a lot of stuff to build our skiff. So what do we really need? A good start would include a saw, hammer, plane, chisel, file, hand drill, a few drill bits, and perhaps some screws and a screwdriver. You will also need something to measure with, perhaps a square for straight lines and a pencil or two. I find it best to work awhile and discover what I need, and then purchase it. This way you won't buy a lot of things that you may never use. Most of the time I get by with twelve or so tools.

This large tool set with over 100 tools contains everything needed to build a wood boat. Compartments lift out and can be carried separately. *Photo by Mark Freeland*

Saws

You will need three cross-cut handsaws of various tooth sizes; two rip saws of various tooth sizes; three frame saws of several tooth sizes; two coping saws, one large and one small; one general purpose hacksaw, and one compass saw for tight curves. You can get by with one good crosscut saw, but a nice hand rip saw is good when ripping planks. *For example, all cuts for the Thoreau boat in this book were made with a common cross-cut toolbox saw from the local do-it-yourself store.*

Hammers

Buy several hammers in various sizes and types. I have one large and one small. A short sledge hammer works well for adjusting stubborn planks and frames and as a backing iron when clenching nails. *The hammer I use the most is a common 16-ounce carpenter's hammer.*

Mallets

I have a large, rubber-covered dead-blow mallet and two wooden mauls, one large and one small, which are used with my good chisels.

Files and wood rasps

An assortment of files and rasps are good to have. For skiff building I use inexpensive horse hoof rasps found at farm stores under equine supplies. These are about a foot in length and have a medium and a coarse cut on opposite sides. These rasps are great for removing lots of wood fast.

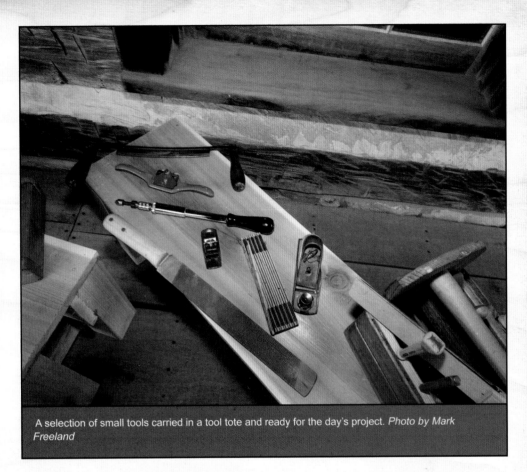

A selection of small tools carried in a tool tote and ready for the day's project. *Photo by Mark Freeland*

Planes

I own about thirty planes, all different kinds and sizes. You can get by with just one plane, but sometimes a specific plane is required. The planes I use the most are my jack plane, smoothing plane, rabbit plane, and block plane. *My favorite is my old Stanley Bailey No. 4 smoothing plane. Planes should be as sharp as you can get them to work correctly.*

Sharpening stones

I have a complete set of oil stones from soft to hard in various shapes and sizes. I do not use mechanical sharpening systems or water stones, though some prefer them. I have one combination stone with medium grit on one side and fine on the other. With honing oil this is all I need to keep my tools usable.

Drivers

A good set of screwdrivers to match the types of fasteners you will use is a necessity. I have three different sized "Yankee"-type mechanical drivers that will accept drill bits, counter sinks, and driver bits.

Chisels

I own a large assortment of chisels of various sizes and quality. I have a set of four fairly short chisels with plastic handles with a steel striking plate. These are my rough work chisels and work well with a steel hammer. These are for the everyday trimming and wood removal. My other set is for hand use or use with the wood mallets. These are honed to razor sharpness and are used for delicate work. I have very sharp carving tools, too. They are used for carving name boards and decorations. There is nothing like a little decoration at the end of a tiller to take it from ordinary to spectacular. Too much fancy stuff on a working skiff is overkill, but just the right amount sets your boat apart.

Boring holes

I have two good hand drills. One is an old egg-beater-type Stanley. The other is a larger hand drill with a chest plate. This one has two speeds and can drill through anything with the correct bit. I also have three different size braces. One is very large and used when boring shaft logs. *For building this little skiff, an egg-beater-style drill works just fine with a few bits to match your fastener sizes.*

Drill bits

Most of the time I only use a few sizes to match the fasteners. I have a good collection of other sizes from small to large along with various auger bits for those times when nothing else will do. Drill bits need to be sharp to work correctly; when buying drill bits, buy good ones. You are really not buying bits, in the end you are buying holes. Better bits bore more holes!

Knives

I have several sizes of draw knives, and spoke shaves, too. These are great for making oars and spars. A good pocket knife is a must for cutting little odd bits, string, scribing a cutting line for sawing, digging out a splinter, and so forth. By the way, go to a medical supply and purchase a good set of tweezers with a machined edge; there's nothing like a good set of tweezers when you need them. While you are at the farm store buying the horse hoof rasps, pick up a hoof knife. Buy both the right-hand and left-hand knives. These are sharp, crooked knives with the tip bent back and hardened. They are great for cleaning out dried glue and stubborn caulking from hard-to-reach crevices. The handles are shaped to fit the hand and are used with a pulling motion.

Clamps

When building most boats, you never have enough clamps; however, with these skiffs, a few will do, because nails and screws are used to hold everything together as you build.

Measuring

I have several tape measures of different lengths and two folding rules in American standard and metric. Two good steel rules are a must, as well, because they take abuse. I love those cheap yardsticks you get at the big box stores. They work great, and in a pinch they make a good shim, too. To these I would add a bevel gauge and a simple plastic protractor. Nothing in a boat is ever really square, but you will need a combination square for cutting boards. Get a few sizes for every contingency. Of course, you can build this boat with nothing but a yardstick and a ball of string. My uncles were always upset with us boys because we kept using their yardsticks for model airplanes and kites. You can never have enough of them around the shop.

There are always extra tools you'll want to throw into your box, such as a set of pliers, an adjustable wrench, awl, center punches and nail sets, several size drifts for reaching hard-to-hit nails, clamps, etc. In skiff-building I use the adjustable wrench mostly for tightening the eyebolt nut for the bow painter line. What I have listed are categories of tools. Start small and add tools as you need them. I often hear, "I need a few power tools; can't I have just one or two, please?" All right: A good battery-operated hand drill is a great time saver and pretty safe, and get a hand jig saw, too. However, the best tool you will ever have is patience.

Edge tools must be sharp to perform. How sharp is sharp? I tell my boat building students to sharpen their tools to the best of their ability. As their sharpening skills improve, they will have sharper tools. The skiffs in this book are primarily built from soft woods like pine, so you can get by with a tool that is less than perfect. About once a year I gather up my plane blades, saws, and chisels, and have them sharpened by a professional sharpening service. The rest of the year all I need to do is tune them up occasionally with a fine stone and a little oil.

You can't just throw edge tools in your tool box and expect them to remain sharp. They are not designed to withstand banging around on other tools. In my box I have specific places for storing my planes, draw knives, spoke shaves, saws, chisels, and drill bits. Buy a tool roll, or at least a box of shop cloths, and wrap your edge tools, and put a little oil on the cloth too. Take good care of your tools, and even the inexpensive ones will perform to your expectations.

That brings up the subject of inexpensive versus expensive tools. Many of my tools are family hand-me-downs, some over 100 years old. In the days when professionals had only hand tools to use, those in trades demanded high-quality steels that were heat-treated to keep a fine edge under hard working conditions, and priced so they could afford them. The marketplace sorted out the poor quality tools from the good tools.

Not so today. Inexpensive power tools are so prevalent now professionals and do-it-yourselfers can use them until they fail, discard them, and buy new ones. The same attitude prevails toward hand tools. Go to any big box store and look over the tools. Most of the brands that were household names and used by professionals and amateurs alike are no longer made in this country. The quality varies a great deal. Does this mean all of these tools are bad? No.

Let's examine the common tools in your boat building tool box. Unless you buy your saws from a specialty tool store, most of the handsaws are now induction hardened. They are very sharp and hold their edges well, but they can't be sharpened again once they leave the factory. When the tool becomes dull, it is discarded.

That goes against my way of thinking, but these saws do work well, and if you take care of them, they will last a long time. Most of the boats in the book were made with saws like these. They are about one tenth of the cost of the type that is intended to be sharpened. That's because the older-style handsaws are now made in limited production quantities. The market no longer sustains large production because almost everyone has switched to power equipment. The same is true of planes, chisels, rasps, and files. You can spend a lot on limited-production hand planes with cast bronze frames and rosewood handles and hand them down through generations. Or you can use the cheaper ones, which probably are finished rough, but can be improved with a little work and sharpening. You can even replace the cheaper blades with better blades made from high-quality steel, and do you really need rosewood handles?

About every three months on a rainy day, I spend a few hours cleaning my tools. This entails scraping off dried glue and paint, oiling, and sharpening. After awhile, rosewood handles look just like the others.

You can purchase a nice tool box to hold your gear, but why not build one yourself? There are many good designs available. Check them out or design your own. Do a good job, and carve your name on it. Many years ago I needed a job between college semesters. Apartments were going up near my house. I picked up my small mahogany tool chest with the leather shoulder strap, walked over, found the site manager, and inquired about work. The first thing he asked me was, "Did you build that tool box?" I answered yes and got a job. The box can define your skill with your craft.

A Place to Build

A shop is as much a state of mind as a real place. My own shop is a little building tucked in a corner of the woods behind my home. It has a shed on the side that allows me to work outside sheltered from the weather, and a deck that provides a large and level work area. In the shop I have a work bench, shelves, and tool cabinets. There is not enough space inside to build a boat much larger than a small dinghy, but I can make all of the subassemblies such as stems, transoms, frames, seats, oars, cleats, knees, and all of the little pieces that every boat needs before it is finished. Then it's outside to work in the shade of a tree, with a picnic table for a work bench and a great view of the valley and creek below.

To build a 16-foot boat inside, I would want a minimum of 4 feet around the boat to allow for working space. Having 6 to 8 feet along one side allows space for a work bench and tools.

A little heat is nice in a cold climate, because glue won't set and paint won't dry in the cold. If you use a lot of power tools you will need a good dust collection system. With hand tools, the shavings and dust fall to the floor where I can sweep them up.

Workbenches

Before you start on the boat, I always suggest building the low benches, sawhorses, and tool and nail tote. These simple projects will provide practice for the more complex tasks to come. The easiest low bench to make is a 2×12-inch by 4-foot-long plank with four 4×4-inch legs, each leg 14 inches long, screwed and glued to the corners of your plank top. If you have trouble cutting wood straight and square, get this material cut at your lumber store. Having the legs cut square and the same length makes it easy. Then all you really need to do is assemble it. With thicker wood you will need no bracing. You will need at least two benches. I usually make a smaller third one to sit on while I work. It saves my back.

Another option is to purchase two sawhorse kits, assemble them per their instructions, but cut the legs down to about 14 inches. Use any leftover wood as braces for the sawhorses. These cheap kits can wobble, and we want our building stands to be steady. Before you make these items, sketch your designs in a notebook. Your sketches will become good references for the future; you can jot down measurements, and when you go to the lumber store you will not forget items.

There are good books on work benches—get them and read them. A long time ago, when I was working in Germany, I purchased a cabinet maker's bench with a complete set of tools and shipped it home. The solid beech bench is 8 feet long and weighs about 400 pounds. It has two side vises and a tail vise with bench dog holes all around. It is a wonderful tool. I also have a smaller bench with caster rollers so I can move it around the shop.

When building small skiffs, the ability to change things around makes the construction easier. I have two portable vises that clamp on makeshift benches. These are great when you need an extra hand to hold something. I also like my heavy-duty state-park-style picnic table outside my shop. I can sit there, work on small parts, and mount my portable vise on the end of the table. I use the table for sketching out ideas, drinking my coffee, and daydreaming about future ideas. When you build a boat, you can dream as much as you want.

Materials

The skiff we will build can be used as a rowboat, motorboat, or sailboat. I call this a multi-use skiff or combination boat. It will be constructed of pine planks, plywood, and a few other materials. Some critics argue that a traditional design must be built entirely of solid wood planks, because plywood was not around 100 years ago. However, to make this book practical for average builders, we will use construction materials found everywhere, and this includes plywood.

A simple 12-foot skiff is a good choice for your first boat. One of the biggest challenges is finding long, high-quality pine planks for the sides. 16-foot planks are standard at most lumber yards, but many home centers do not stock that length in some dimensions. A way around this situation is to use shorter planks and join them end to end. Most of the skiffs of this type were around 12 to 20 feet long, 4 to 6 feet wide, and about 2 feet deep; the shorter the skiff, the smaller the overall size for everything.

These skiffs were originally built with pine, cedar, cypress, sassafras, tulip poplar, and other local native woods. I like to use white cedar for planking and longleaf yellow pine for the stem, spreader stick, frames, and seats. Sometimes I use plain #2 pine because it is always available.

The following materials list is typical for our project.

- 4 #2 or better 1×12-inch planks, 12 feet long
- 8 trim sticks 1×2-inch, 12 feet long (often called screen stock)
- 1 14-foot piece of ¾×¾-inch trim stock. This will be used as a limber batten to draw long, even, sheer curves on the side planks. Later the wood can be used as short braces or trim stock for a splash rail.
- 2 or more #2 common or better 2×4's, 10 feet long
- 3 sheets of ⅜-inch 4×8-foot marine plywood

- 1 partial sheet of ¾-inch marine plywood, 2 feet by 4 feet, used for the transom. Marine plywood is expensive; however, it is very durable and in my opinion worth the money. For your first build you can substitute good-quality exterior grade plywood if you wish. It will not last as long as marine grade, but it is a lower-cost alternative.
- 1 16-ounce bottle of water-resistant PVA glue
- 1 quart of below-the-waterline-grade bedding compound Use Dolfinite® bedding compound made by the Pettit Paint Co. or an equivalent

- 1 box of 2-inch #8 hot-dipped galvanized nails
- 1 box of 1½-inch #6 hot-dipped galvanized nails
- 1 box of aluminum vinyl siding ring shank nails with large heads for attaching the plywood bottom
- If you choose to use screws, you will need at least one box of 2-inch epoxy-coated all-weather fasteners used for decks, barns, and outside projects.

Adhesives

I use water-resistant PVA (polyvinyl acetate) glue for gluing little bits on the boat and laminating above the waterline. One of the most common adhesives on the market, these are often referred to as yellow wood glues. They are not waterproof, although come pretty close and the chemists are improving them constantly. Some are more water-resistant than others. Read the labels, and never be stingy with glue. It isn't worth it.

Resorcinol-type glue meets the Navy's rigorous testing for waterproofing. This urea formaldehyde glue is toxic and must be handled with care. This is wonderful glue, but it is becoming more difficult to find, many stores are not carrying it anymore, and I have quit using it. Water resistant PVA glues meet my needs just fine. They clean up with water before they dry and are safe and inexpensive.

Wood

If you don't want to use 1×12-inch planks, you can always use narrower material and adjust accordingly. Regarding wood quality, #2 common pine is okay. Look for boards with the fewest knots, and leave the split planks on the stack.

Fasteners

One hundred years ago, boat builders used plain iron or hot-dipped galvanized iron nails. They could be clinched (bent over) or unclinched, depending on the construction technique. Today you can find many types of hot-dipped galvanized nails, and other fasteners, too. The galvanized nails are steel rather than iron today, but they will work for our skiffs. Real hot-dipped galvanized steel boat nails can be special ordered, but are very expensive.

I try to keep fastener types and sizes to my own common standard to reduce the number of odd batches. For most of my skiffs I use #6 and #8 hot-dipped galvanized nails in lengths appropriate to the plank thicknesses I am building with. A 2-inch nail will work for most jobs. Throw in screws of various sizes, and occasionally some other fasteners, and that's about it.

Fasteners

Start with a box or two. You can always get more as you need them. In fifth grade, my daughter made me a little tool tote in shop class. It has six compartments where I keep different size fasteners. This is a handy accessory that I use on every boat build. I used to wear a carpenter's tool belt, but the extra weight has caused me some pain over the years.

Paint

The pine wood sold today is not of the quality it once was and will last longer if you paint it or coat it with wood preservative. Acrylics (latex paints) do a good job and dry much faster than oil-based coatings such as marine paint, and they clean up with soap and water. If I use acrylics, I choose the industrial grades designed for harsh environments. Their surface film is usually harder than paints for home use.

No matter what anyone tells you, varnish does not hold up well outside. If I varnish anything on these skiffs it might be a few bits of trim and small decorative pieces. A little varnish on an old work boat design is fine, but too much does not look right, in my opinion. However, if a client wants a varnished boat, I will use at least six coats, sanding between each coat with extra-fine sandpaper.

Traditional oil finishes such as boiled linseed oil mixed with pine tar always look smart. Traditional paint schemes for these boats were pretty simple. For example, they might be black on the bottom, green on the hull, light gray or an oiled finish inside, and have a red boot-top stripe at the waterline.

I do a lot of thinking before I decide which type of skiff to build next. I sketch ideas and discard most of them. So, take a break at this point, put your feet up and rest a bit. Here is a true skiff tale from another era that defines flatiron working skiffs and the people who used them.

Little Jonah and the Hurricane

I am often asked why I build wooden boats and what is so special about them. These aren't easy questions to answer. Let's just say skiff building allows me to not only explore the designs, but explore the history as well. It is not all about building, either. It is about using these boats for fun, imagining what it would be like to work without motors, relying on the wind and muscle power.

For example, last summer we won a race or two, didn't come in last every time, and no one got injured. Autumn entered with a flurry of color and November came easy. I had finally caught up most of my projects, and then a close friend got married and brought all of his boat stuff over to my place. An early gift for the holidays, he said. I grumbled, but gave in and said I could probably make room somewhere, and helped him unload his trailer. One old spruce mast and boom were released from the clutches of at least a dozen rotted bungee cords, bags of miscellaneous hardware and rope, and a once-good sail that had been used as a painter's drop cloth. The big prize, though, was an unfinished 11-foot dinghy. He said he wouldn't need these things anymore. He had other priorities.

A month has passed and I've just finished packing it all away. A few light snowflakes drift passed the shop window. The sky is the color of fresh-cut steel, but here in the workshop it is warm. I take another look at this dinghy that Nick dropped off at my place. It is a Charles Wittholz design, a cat rig for rowing or sailing, a nice little boat for a winter project. For the past hour I have been sitting in my chair staring at the transom. Right after breakfast I penciled in a name, shaded it and everything, so I could get some idea what it would look like when completed.

What's in a name anyway? I've often wondered how boats get their names. When I go to marinas and walk the docks, each one tells some kind of story. Some names are easy to figure out—wives, girlfriends, exotic names of faraway places, and sometimes egocentric ones.

The previous summer, for instance, I was working in New York City and had been watching the boats sail out of Rockaway Harbor. I asked one of the local guys building new docks where I could rent a boat for the day, or perhaps find a ride for an afternoon sail. Peter asked me a few questions and then put down his tools and said. "I don't know where you can rent boats, but I know a real sailor who might. My grandfather is almost ninety, but until about five years ago he ran a sailing program not far from here."

I agreed to meet him. They lived on Staten Island in the house his grandfather had built. The next day as we crossed the bridge to the island, I tried to imagine an older New York, when all the boats were either wood or iron plate, and working sail was already giving way to boats with engines. We made a sharp turn, and the neat brick row houses on both sides of the street formed a little secluded canyon. The noise of the city disappeared as we stepped into the entry.

Peter's grandfather sat in the parlor. He stood up and held out his hand. It was twice the size of mine and his smile grew into a big grin. We said a few words about the weather and my work. Peter headed off to the kitchen to make lunch and said, "Pop, tell him about the storm of 1938."

The old fellow sat straight in his chair by the window, looking out past the curtains and cars. The sunlight grew brighter and the old lace curtains cast patterns in the room. Then he looked straight at me, his blue eyes and Norwegian heritage betraying the New York accent. He began his story.

"It was September and summer was already gone. I was twenty-five years old. The days were getting shorter. It must have been about two in the afternoon and all of us down at the club realized that this storm, that had started with a light rain out of the north two days before, wasn't going to be like any of the others that had come through this year. We had a glass in the office and it hadn't stopped falling all day. We were told to go out and bring in all of the little boats that were on buoys and double chain the two big yachts in the harbor. The harbormaster said we were really in for a blow.

"We took the club launch out to the boats and the three of us worked like madmen trying to beat the storm. We had the last four boats in tow and were heading back, when one of the boys heard a dog barking. I turned and saw a piece of white fluff leap into the water. Someone had left a little dog on one of the big yachts. It had made its way down the yacht's ladder, and now it was swimming for us. Every now and then we could catch a glimpse of it in the waves as our launch crashed up and down. We all knew the dog wouldn't make it. Our launch was having a rough time of it in the wind, let alone towing the boats.

"We were better than halfway to the club pier, and I couldn't expect the boys to turn back to rescue the dog. I told them to take the launch back to the club and I'd go get the dog in one of the skiffs we were towing. We were only a thousand yards from the shore. I'd pick up the dog and drift back. Then they could get me."

The old sailor took a bite of his sandwich, sipped some water, and slumped back into his chair. Fatigue shot through him, and then he leaned forward and looked at us.

"We have maybe one chance in our lives to do one good thing, and if you don't take it, that chance may never come again."

I could feel the emotion in his speech. The tone of his voice changed and a cloud dampened the sunlight in the room. He went on.

"I don't know what makes some dogs do what they do, but when I started to row toward it, the dog turned around and started to go back to the boat it had just left. I knew I had no choice now; the dog wouldn't be able to get back up the yacht's ladder, and it would never have the endurance to swim to shore.

"I put all of my strength into it and pulled that flatiron skiff until I thought my arms would come right out of my shoulders. Finally I caught up with the dog, reached down, grabbed it and heaved the little bit of fur into the skiff. I spun the oars, turned the boat around, and headed back to the club. The dog went under the seat and hid, and I looked up and saw the sky for the first time. It had turned an ugly greenish black, and it was raining sideways. The wind direction had changed, too, and was blowing harder. I could see that all the rowing in the world wouldn't get us back to land. I looked at the dog and said, `You're some little Jonah, aren't you?' The dog just looked at me and shook.

"Somehow I got the mast and sail up; maybe with the sail we could make a little headway. Our skiff busted through the waves and water flew all around us. The wind kept coming like a sea-going freight train late for its next stop. The skiff had an ash mast, probably made from an old oar, with a scrap of tarp for a sail. The wind would clobber us and the mast would bend at the bow seat. Just when I thought it would snap right in two we would clear a wave top and slam down into another trough. I was using one of the oars as a rudder, and I had to hang on to it for dear life to keep it from coming out of the sculling socket. I talked to the dog to keep my courage up. It wouldn't come out from under the seat, and that was just as well, because with the way we were being tossed around, I was afraid he'd try to jump out. I was scared too, and couldn't think about anything except keeping us upright and moving toward shore.

"Maybe the rain let up some, I can't remember, but we made the floating pier at the end of the club house. The yard crew met us with two boat hooks and snagged the skiff as it went charging by. Safely out of the weather and in the club office, we watched several boats from another pier float out of sight. The storm was really kicking up a fuss. I thought we had been in that mess for only a few minutes, but they told me later that we'd been out in it for better than an hour. The boys and the harbormaster had tried to go back and get us, but the old launch engine was missing out so badly they didn't know if it would make it one more time.

"The owners picked up the dog later that day. Don't think I ever learned its real name, we were all too busy tying everything down to talk to them, and besides, back then yacht owners never talked much to yard boys. The storm blew more rain and wind and turned into a pretty bad hurricane, but I don't think

I've ever felt better for what I did that afternoon."

After lunch, Peter and I went back to work. He said he had heard this story many times since he was a child, and never tired of it. Sometimes the details would change a bit, but it was always good just the same. I finished my work and headed home. I never did get to go sailing in New York, at least not on that trip anyway, but it didn't matter. I had fun and learned some things. Months later I received a letter saying Peter's grandfather had passed on, along with a nice obit telling how he had been a New York Harbor tugboat captain and a decorated naval officer in World War II. The family had sold the Staten Island house and relocated outside the big city. I was curious, so I looked up past hurricanes, the big destructive ones. On September 21, 1938, a massive storm with winds exceeding 100 miles an hour hit New England and more than 600 people were killed.

So here I sit in my shop looking at this dinghy. The design has a real fine shape with a delicate turn at the bilge. I measure the letters once more, shove another stick of wood in the stove, and ask my cat for a second opinion. No answer. Cats are so noncommittal.

With my good brush I begin to paint the words Little Jonah with a gentle arc across the stern. I'll varnish and gold-leaf it in the spring when the weather is warmer and I can work with the doors open. I'll paint the rest of the boat a light green color like I always do, and in the summer when my friends at the sailing club ask what's with the name, I'll probably shrug my shoulders and say, "Now there's a story."

2

Building the Skiff

Our build schedule divides the tasks into simple steps. This book is designed to walk you through those steps and explain why you are doing certain things as you progress toward completion. Take things slow; there is no reason to hurry.

Building a Model

A paper construction model for a 12-foot skiff; the model provides a preview of the finished boat. Color choices, seat arrangements, trim, and other ideas can be tried out on a model before building the actual boat. The scale is 1 inch to the foot.

Unless you have some experience with woodworking, and some knowledge of boat building, I suggest building a model first. Its primary purpose is to preview the fitting and assembly of the parts. This "practice boat" will give you the advantage of learning where things might go wrong and be ready when it happens. If you spend time making the skiff model, you will save a week or more of frustration, and learn a lot, too. Trust me on this one. They are not intended to be display models, although they could be if you take extra care when you build them.

Not long ago, small boat shops built working boats such as lobster and crab skiffs by eye from models whittled out of a block of sugar pine or other soft wood. The hull shape could be taken off and transferred to a drawing, and then to full-size patterns, or just used as a guide. Take out your notebook and draw up some ideas. Transfer those ideas to your model. With the model you can try out different transom sizes, deck and seat combinations, and color schemes.

The model does not have to be perfectly to scale, but we need to get enough of it correct that we can understand how everything goes together. In other words, we need to get the important measurements correct. One easy way is to build a model 1 inch to the foot. If you are making a 12-foot boat, the model would be 12 inches long.

I try to find little bits of wood and cardboard I can use for materials. If you can't find perfect scale model material, just get as close as you can. Build the model in the same order as the real boat. Go so far as to make two benches for the boat to rest on while you are building.

You can always build a larger model too. During the early part of the twentieth century, there were several boat companies building high quality skiffs, canoes, and other types of small boats that were sold all over the United States. Most of these were intended for sportsmen who would use them for hunting or fishing. Unlike the common working craft of the period, these were finished out with nice paint schemes, varnish, and woven cane seats. The boats came with good bronze hardware and first-class oars. A variety of these boats would be made in a smaller scale to simplify shipping for display in stores far away from the manufacturer.

A 16-foot boat display model would be about 4 feet long. Today these display models, some over 100 years old, fetch a good sum on the antiques market. A family-run sporting goods store near me has one. I have tried to buy it over the years, but they won't part with it. I can't blame them. It is a work of art.

The best models are the larger ones, because they provide more information and are easier to make than smaller sizes. The 1-inch-to-the-foot models are easy to calculate, but sometimes they are too small to get a good feel for how planks bend and seats and braces fit. Larger models also give you a good a sense of proportion for the rigging, spars, sails, and other parts required for sailing. I have even used small figurines to gain a better understanding of how people would use the boat.

These larger models make great toys for small children, for making imaginary voyages around their bedrooms. If you want to build a larger model, please do so. For planks you can use ¼-inch plywood, and for 2×4's you can use small trim wood. If children are going to play with it, make it strong and get them involved in building it, too.

Building the Five Subassemblies

The flatiron skiff design we are building is constructed from five major subassemblies: the stem, transom, spreader stick, lower and upper side planks, and bottom. For other design variations, these subassemblies would still need to be made. They will all be similar; whether you are building a model or the actual boat. However, the dimensions will change. As your skills improve, you can make more changes as you wish. If this is your first boat build, please follow the instructions as closely as possible.

Even though we do not have plans, you can make a few simple plans to use as a guide until you become familiar with building by eye. Using this technique, you train yourself to visualize a component and build it as you imagine it. There is no need to be a great artist. Do your best.

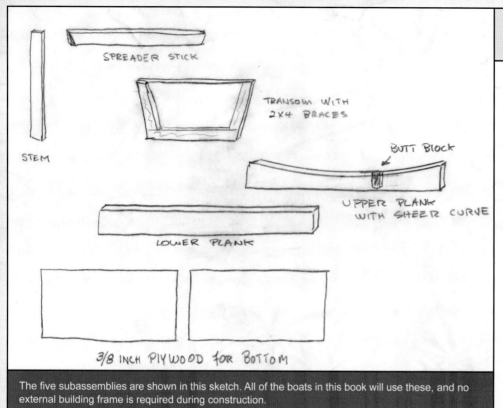

SPREADER STICK

TRANSOM WITH
2X4 BRACES

STEM

BUTT BLOCK

UPPER PLANK
WITH SHEER CURVE

LOWER PLANK

3/8 INCH PLYWOOD FOR BOTTOM

The five subassemblies are shown in this sketch. All of the boats in this book will use these, and no external building frame is required during construction.

Subassembly One: Stem

The bow is the front of the boat, and the stem makes up the bow. For our skiff, a primary front structural part is the stem and can be made from a single piece of wood, or several. We will use only one piece of wood. Cut a 2×4 to 30 inches in length. This is your stem subassembly and will be trimmed to fit when we begin to assemble the hull. Set this aside for now.

Subassembly Two: Transom

The stern is the back of the boat, and the structure that makes up the stern is called the transom. It can be a single piece of plywood or several planks fastened together. Dimensions will vary depending on the size or type of skiff. For example, if you are building a 12-foot skiff, the transom width at the top could be anywhere from 30 inches to 38 inches wide or even larger. Making the transom narrow compared to the beam adds a long curve to the after-section of

the hull; however, a very narrow transom will require aggressive plank bending.

With our skiffs, the curve created by the stem, spreader stick, and transom is often referred to as a fish form. A long time ago, people figured out that if boats were shaped like fish, they would probably go through the water pretty well.

If you look at a fish from a top you will see the shape. It is a little blunt and rounded at

the front and tapers toward the back, creating a fine exit for water flow at the tail of the fish. Our boat will take a variation of this shape. If you plan on using an outboard motor, a wider transom will support more weight aft. In my boat building classes, I often build skiffs with wide transoms for this very reason. This makes bending the side planks into place easier as well, and if you choose to convert the outboard boat to a sailboat or rowboat later, it will still

An outside transom view looking forward with the lower and upper planks in place. You can see the stringers that provide extra material for fastening the planks to each other. The skiff is resting on two low benches that provide a comfortable working height.

Inside view of a transom with the lower and upper planks in place. This transom is made from solid wood planks edge glued with braces for support. A sculling hole accommodates a sculling oar. Sculling is a single oar technique used for quiet propulsion. The action is similar to a tail fin on a fish.

perform okay. A narrow dimension at the bottom of the transom forces more curve into the hull planks and creates flare, which results in a rocker shape on the bottom.

Outboard motors sized to fit this skiff should be low-horsepower; five or even less is plenty, and the motor should weigh no more than 50 or so pounds. With a person sitting in the back of the boat and steering the motor, add another 250 pounds. We want the back of the boat to easily support 350 pounds or more. A wider transom designed for a motor supports this weight by providing more volume in the back of the boat.

In this example, we are laying out a 38-inch-wide transom using ¾ -inch plywood. I prefer marine grade, but quality exterior grade will work fine. Your 12-foot skiff will need only a quarter sheet, 24×48 inches, of this thicker plywood for the transom. Most home lumber stores sell plywood cut to this size. Lay out, mark, and cut the plywood panel to 24 inches by 38 inches. Set the leftover piece of plywood aside; we will use it for other parts later.

Next, we will lay out our transom angle. This angle will determine the amount of twist in our side planks. Remember, twist will create flare in the boat hull. Flare adds volume to the boat; it also adds a pleasing curve and a little rocker to the bottom and provides overall stability to the hull. A transom that is narrower at the bottom than the top will add more twist to the planks and slightly more flare to the hull.

Transom angles for skiffs are often arbitrary, but here is an easy method for figuring it out: Place your panel so the 38-inch width is at the top. At the bottom of the rectangle, measure inward 2 inches on each side and then draw a straight pencil line from the bottom measurement to the top corner. If you measure in 3 inches from each side you will add more twist to your side planks and more flare to the boat. If you left your transom square to the top and bottom, your skiff would be slab-sided, or straight up and down. A lot of skiffs were once built slab-sided. They weren't very pretty, but they were functional and quick to make. These were often used as barges to haul stone, sand, coal, and other rough cargo.

Using your saw, cut the angles you have drawn. Save the scraps for later use.

The next step in building the transom is to add three braces. These will be made from 2×4s trimmed to fit the transom shape on the bottom and two sides. The transom with the braces will be mounted inside the boat. Fasten the braces to the plywood with PVA glue and nails. Nail through the plywood and into the 2×4 braces. Always wipe off any remaining glue with a damp cloth before it dries. Set the transom aside and let the glue dry completely.

When the transom is installed on the boat and both side planks are attached, you can trim the top of the transom to the desired shape. This boat's transom is 24 inches from bottom to top. The two side planks will be 21 inches high, leaving approximately 3 inches to leave as is or to trim away. You can trim the top of the transom in several ways. One way is to draw a curve from the right to the left side just above each top plank. Cut along the line, and the transom will have a nice arc. This will take some of the boxy look away from the skiff. Do this after the side planks are installed.

If you decide to use a small outboard, trim the top of the transom to fit the motor. Most small motors require a 15-inch transom height from the mount to the water. However, this is not always the case. The cavitation plate on the motor above the propeller needs to be under the water. I always wait and cut the transom to fit the motor.

Subassembly Three: Spreader Stick

The spreader stick in position on the two lower planks. The spreader stick determines the boat's width, or beam. At the end of the plank you can see a positioning cleat for attaching the transom and creating the transom rake. *Photo by Mark Freeland*

The spreader stick is a simple but important part of the boat construction, because it is a primary frame for establishing the width of the boat. Along with the transom, it creates the flare that gives the boat increased volume and pleasing lines.

The spreader stick is a 40-inch-long 2×4 with an angle cut on each end to match the transom angle. A larger boat would have a longer spreader to make the hull wider. For example, a 16-foot boat could have a spreader stick 46 to 60 inches or longer.

Lay your transom on top of the spreader stick and mark the angle of the spreader stick. You want the spreader stick angle to be the same as the transom. During construction, the spreader stick begins the twist of the side planks. When the side planks are attached to

the transom, this twist is anchored into a permanent shape at the transom. The twist stiffens the hull. As other pieces are added to the boat hull, the whole assembly will become more rigid and stronger. Strength is achieved through the sum of the parts.

Fasten the spreader stick into position using one nail on each side. The final assembly will use two nails per side to control twisting of the spreader during transom assembly. *Photo by Mark Freeland*

Subassembly Four: Lower and Upper Side Planks

What remains now is to measure and shape the side planks so they will fit onto the stem, transom, and each other. The side planks can be a little confusing. If you made your model, much of the confusion will be eliminated, and if you are following the instructions now for making a model, follow closely, because it is really quite simple.

For the lower plank sides, start by choosing the two best 1×12-inch, 12-foot-long boards from your stock. If there are any edge knots, put them on the top where they will be covered by the upper planks. Mark top and bottom and front and back with a pencil as well as inside and outside. In this way you will not forget which side is correct for your assembly. Also, this is why I like models so much, because you

The lower and upper planks are attached to the bow stem and transom, which is not shown. The middle seat is on top of the spreader stick for fitting. When assembled, the spreader stick becomes a seat brace and structural member tying the boat halves together.

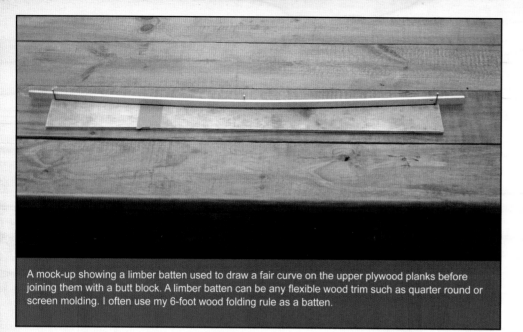

A mock-up showing a limber batten used to draw a fair curve on the upper plywood planks before joining them with a butt block. A limber batten can be any flexible wood trim such as quarter round or screen molding. I often use my 6-foot wood folding rule as a batten.

can have your model marked in this way and follow your model as you lay out your boards. After you have chosen and marked your lower planks, set them aside and start on the upper planks.

Using 12-foot boards, your boat will be about 11 feet, 6 inches long because the curve of the planks will reduce the length. You can always purchase longer boards to make your boat exactly 12 feet or perhaps 13 feet long. You can cut off the remaining plank wood later and use it for seats or a deck. Sometimes builders are really surprised when they finish their boat and it is not exactly 12 feet in length. Now is the time to make this adjustment if you wish.

The upper side planks will be made from ⅜-inch marine plywood. By the way, this boat can be made entirely from solid wood or plywood; however, with this example we will use ply on the top planks, so you can learn to work with it. I will discuss other construction options in more detail later. Thin plywood is easy to bend and lighter-weight than solid planks. This is why we are going to use it for our upper planking.

To make the upper planks, cut one of your 4×8 sheets of plywood into four planks length-wise. The plywood planks will be approximately 1 foot wide, less the width of a saw blade, and 8 feet long. You can have this cut at your lumber store; many stores will do this free of charge.

If you choose to cut it yourself, lay out four straight lines and use your cross-cut handsaw or a power saw. After you cut four panels, cut one in half and lay it on the floor end to end with one of the 8-foot panels. When they are joined you will have a 12-foot plank, the same as the lower planks, but made from plywood.

The next step is to lay out the sheer curve and cut it. Put the 8-foot and 4-foot panels together end to end and temporarily fasten them together with tape. The tape is used to hold the two plywood pieces while you measure and mark them. We will use the long 14-foot limber batten, which is ¾-inch square, to lay out our curve onto the plywood. Measure 6 feet from either end of the temporarily joined panels to find the center and make a pencil mark. Then measure down 2 inches and make a mark. Drive a small nail on this mark, and another small nail at the end of each panel in the top corner; three nails total. These will hold your batten in place while you draw your curve. To do this, spring the batten under the middle nail and over the tops of the end nails. Use a pencil to mark the curved line on the outside of the batten. This will become the sheer line on your skiff. Cut along the line with your handsaw or power jigsaw. Then mark the panels so you will not become confused as to which side is right or left. Repeat this procedure for your other upper plank. Save the remaining plywood for later use.

Making and using butt blocks to join the plywood panels end to end

A mock-up showing butt block attachment for joining the upper planks together. Note the position of the butt block to allow for the lap of the upper planks over the lower.

The butt blocks will be made from the leftover ¾-inch plywood you used for the transom. Measure the width of the plywood panel at the joint from top to bottom. It should be about 9 inches or so wide. Then measure from the bottom of the panel (the straight side) up two inches and make a mark. Cut your leftover ¾-inch plywood into two pieces 6 inches wide and about 1 foot in length for the butt blocks. Any extra material can be trimmed later. Remove your temporary tape at this time. Take one of the butt blocks and place it on the mark at 2 inches from the bottom. The reason the butt blocks do not cover the complete plank width is to allow for a 2-inch overlap of the upper planks over the bottom planks. This is called "lap strake" construction and makes a strong joint; when we assemble the boat, this lap joint will become more apparent.

Join the two planks using the butt blocks with glue and nails or screws, and set aside to dry for twenty-four hours. Always fasten from the thinner material to the thicker material when possible. In other words the fasteners for the butt blocks will be placed from the outside of the ⅜-inch ply toward the inward ¾-inch ply.

There is a simple way to make this job easier. Spread glue on the butt block, place it into position, and tape it so it doesn't move. I use blue painter's tape. Carefully flip the joined plank over and screw or nail the butt block. Once the glue has set, most of the holding power comes from the glue; however, I am always overbuilding things a bit and I like plenty of mechanical fasteners.

Where the butt block joint is located on a boat can determine its longevity. They will be placed toward the aft or rear of the boat, where there will be few radical bends in the planks. In the days of the wooden Navy, huge butt blocks of hardwood were used to join huge planks. They were often bolted into place, with bedding compound between the joints. If the ship's planks were a bit green, and many times they were, the butt block bolts could be tightened as the wood dried out. We will not need to do this on the skiffs we build.

Subassembly Five: Bottom

The bottom is the major subassembly of our skiff. We will fit the bottom during the assembly procedure of the boat. Therefore, set your two full ⅜-inch plywood sheets aside for now.

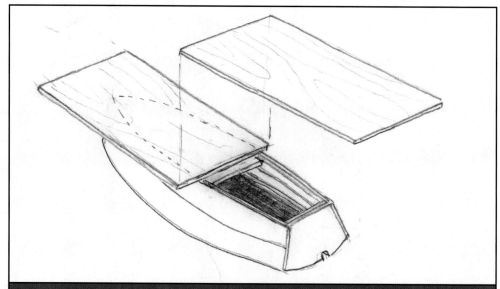

This sketch shows positioning the two pieces of plywood for the boat's bottom. Note the bottom butt block and combination spreader stick arrangement. This will tie the bottom boat halves together and provide attachment points for the forward and rear bottom panels.

Assembling the Pieces and Building the Skiff

This is where we start assembling pieces and turning them into a boat. If you have a helper on the first assembly day, the tasks go pretty quickly; otherwise, have patience and go slowly. Always think through each step before starting. For example, with help, attaching the stem, two bottom planks, spreader stick, and transom should take no more than one day.

The good news is once the above is completed you will have a boat shape. Everything else will follow from this. This technique allows the builder to make the boat in layers. You continue adding parts until it is complete. Unlike working from specific plans, building by eye allows great flexibility with the construction. You can change things around if you wish as long as you keep the basic design within the framework you have already completed. In this case, the framework is the stem, spreader stick, side planks, and transom. These make the hull shape. You can make the seats larger or smaller, add a seat or take one away, add storage, change the deck configuration, make the final boat for use with a motor, rowing, a sail, or do all three if you wish.

Keep in mind basic rules of carpentry. Measure several times before cutting. When trimming to fit, cut away small amounts of material until the piece you are working on slips easily into place. Never force things; bending planks to shape is one thing, but trying to make something fit when the dimension is incorrect will only lead to problems and material failure.

Step 1: Determining Transom Rake

Fitting the transom to the Thoreau boat, inside view. The transom cleats make it easy to position the transom to a predetermined transom rake. A helper is holding the transom while the builder holds it in place with a cord prior to fastening. *Photo by Mark Freeland*

A transom on a traditional 16-foot rowing boat with a sculling hole reinforced by the carved name board. The boat is on the Indianapolis, Indiana, Central Canal, where it is used as a rental for rowers.

Transom rake is the angle of the transom. A straight up and down transom would be 90 degrees to the perpendicular. In other words, the back of the boat is straight up and down in relation to the bottom of the boat. We can build our transom like this; however, for this design it will look better to the eye if we increase the angle to about 95 degrees or a little more. This does two things. The angle is more pleasing to the eye, and when using a small outboard motor it helps to prevent the wake that the boat creates as it goes through the water from splashing back into the boat. Don't worry about angles; there is an easy way to do this.

The next step is to mark your right and left-side planks so the laps will be even and look correct. The easiest way to do this is to lay the planks out flat with the bottom plank overlapping the top plank by 2 inches. When you do this, you will be seeing the planks as you would from the inside of the boat. Use the

Looking aft to the transom shows how the spreader stick in conjunction with the transom angle twists the planks and creates flare to the hull. Note the curved deck example made from walnut and cherry wood. The bottom is not installed at this time.

An outside view installing the transom on the Thoreau boat; the cleats on the inside position the transom rake. The transom angles along with the spreader stick determine the hull flare. A cord holds the side planks into place prior to fastening. *Photo by Mark Freeland*

butt block as a guide. It will extend 2 inches over the bottom plank. With a pencil, mark the lap along the full length of your top plank. When it is time to install the top plank, all you will need to do is match the line to your bottom plank. During installation, the lap may not come out perfect as the plank bends. The front of the boat may be a little different from the back. This is why we use a 2-inch lap, because there is plenty of room to make adjustments. Don't worry about it. The most important thing is to do your best and make both sides of the boat look as even as possible.

Next move to the back of the boat; this will be the end closest to the butt block joint if you

Two skiff models show a comparison of transom rake. The model on the left is a rowing boat with an extreme rake, and the model on the right is a combination boat that can be rowed, powered with a small outboard, or sailed. The rake on the combination boat is about 5 degrees.

have done everything correctly. From the top of the upper rear plank, measure in 3 inches and make a mark; from the bottom corner of the lower plank, measure in 4 inches and make a mark, and then use a straight edge and pencil to draw a line between the two marks.

As a reminder, we put the butt blocks toward the rear of these skiffs because the curve is more gradual and the joint is not stressed as much. On some designs we can place the butt blocks in the front, where they will be hidden under the deck.

The line you just drew defines your transom rake. If you want a little more rake, measure in 5 inches on the bottom. Remove the top plank and set it aside. Make sure it is marked right or left so you don't confuse it with the other side. Now cut a piece of 1×2-inch trim stock and glue and nail it to the inside of the line on the bottom plank. The nails hold everything together until the glue dries. Make sure the nails do not come through the outside of the plank. Cut the stock a little long; you can trim it later. Repeat the step for the other side. These locating cleats establish the transom rake and make the assembly of the transom easy. An easy way to make sure the nails do not come through is to nail them in at an angle. There is little stress on these cleats.

Step 2: Joining the Two Lower Planks at the Bow

We will start joining the two bottom planks in the front at the stem area. I call this procedure my soup can method. Cut out the top and bottom of a coffee or soup can. Use tin snips to cut the can so you have a small piece of sheet metal, and then flatten it out. Punch two holes about 1 inch from each end, four holes total. Bend the metal into a V shape and attach the two bottom planks with screws. The easiest way to do this is on your benches or a flat floor.

The sheet metal acts like a hinge to allow the hull planks to bend and seek their own correct angle. The final stem angle is determined by the spreader stick in conjunction with the transom. The sheet metal hinge will hold the front of the boat together while we position the spreader stick and attach the transom. The can material will be removed later.

Instead of the sheet metal, I have used heavy duct tape, electrical twist ties, suspended ceiling wire, and nails. I like the tin can method the best, because it holds the planks into position better than the other methods.

Cut the soup can after both ends have been removed. *Photo by Mark Freeland*

Join the two hull planks using the "soup can method." With a flattened soup can temporarily holding the hull planks together, the spreader and transom can be fitted and fastened. The actual stem will be installed later. *Photo by Mark Freeland*

Flatten the can to make a small piece of sheet metal. *Photo by Mark Freeland*

Punch four holes in the can for screws. *Photo by Mark Freeland*

The two lower planks are placed on top of each other and the soup can is shaped over the ends of the planks. *Photo by Mark Freeland*

The soup can is attached with four screws, two on each side. The screws are being driven into the planks with a Yankee screwdriver, also referred to as an automatic screwdriver or push drill. In the background is the Thoreau boat with three cedar clapboard planks on each side. *Photo by Mark Freeland*

Step 3: Attaching the Spreader Stick

For a 12-foot boat, measure approximately 5 feet back from the temporary hinge piece and lay the spreader stick between the side planks. Visualize how it will work and make a mark at the top of the planks. This mark must be the same on each side of your boat. If you built your model, you will know how it works. You want the planks to begin bending slightly forward of the middle of the boat. On a larger boat, place the spreader stick slightly forward of the middle. For example, on a 16-foot skiff, the spreader stick would be 7 feet back from the hinge piece. By doing this, you will begin to create the fish form we discussed earlier.

Now, mark the side planks at the top and attach the spreader stick to the planks. It is smart to drill pilot holes for your fasteners here. The angle you previously cut on the spreader stick will begin to shape and flare the boat hull. Combined with the transom angle, this will twist the planks. Attach the spreader stick with screws or nails. Fasten each side with one fastener first. You don't want the fasteners to be tight in the beginning; the planks need to be flexible when you are attaching the transom. You will use two fasteners on each side when completed. There will be a fair amount of stress on the planks as you bend and twist them to shape. Bend slowly, and have patience. Bend the wood several times, each time a little more. This flexes the wood fibers. After the transom is attached, everything can be tightened up. There is no need for glue on the ends of the spreader stick. When the transom is installed, everything will be held in tension.

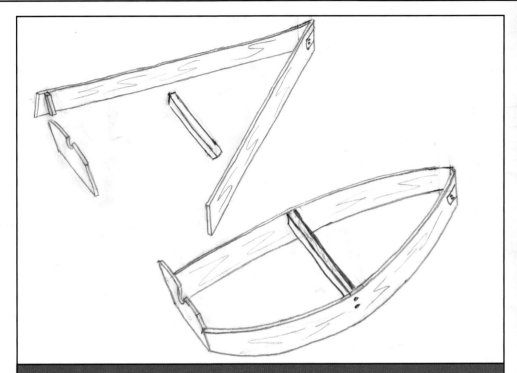

This sketch shows the plank assemblies to create the boat shape using the soup can with two lower side planks, spreader stick, and transom.

I have never had a dry-bend fail with these dimensions. However, if you are reluctant to dry-bend your side planks, here is another method I have used, but don't try this unless dry-bending fails. Several weeks before you start your boat build, put the low benches you made outside where the weather can work its magic. Wet your planks and place them over the benches, holding them down with bricks or cement blocks. Soak them good with water each night or let the rain wet them and the sun dry them. Leave the boards out in the weather for at least two weeks. When you get ready to use them, they will be bent. Make sure you pick the sides for left and right; once the planks have taken a weather set, you will not be able to bend them back the other way.

Never bend plywood this way, because it might warp. If you need a little extra help when bending plywood, hot towels will usually do the trick.

Step 4: Installing the Transom

When installing the transom, think through the process as you did on the model; having help can speed things up but it is not required. The locating cleats you previously installed will help to align the planks and transom with the correct transom rake. First, bend the two planks together as they would need to be when fitting the transom, and feel the planks stiffen as you pull them together. You can even over-bend it an inch or two several times to flex the wood fibers. You should not have to wet the wood. Take your time. You will hear the wood make some noises, and that is okay.

When you have the planks into position to accept the transom assembly, spread bedding compound on the transom sides and the back side of the locating cleats for a good seal. This is messy stuff, but it can be cleaned easily with a little mineral spirits and makes a good watertight bond. Wear rubber gloves and old clothes or a shop apron. Now, wrap a cord around the planks a few times to hold them into position. The rope loop technique that uses a turning stick to draw the planks together is called a Spanish Windlass and has been used in all types of construction since ancient times. The cord can be tightened or loosened to allow for positioning the transom against the locating cleats. The cleats establish the transom rake we previously determined. Tighten everything up with the cord before fastening the assembly.

Look it over and make sure it is square with the rest of the planks; if the transom looks crooked in relation to the front, it will need to be adjusted. Measure from each top corner of

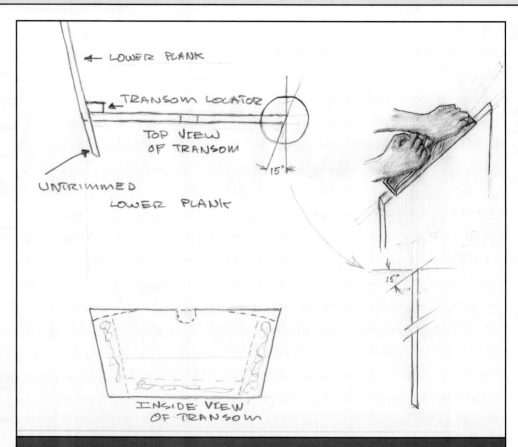

This sketch shows the relationship of the side planks to the transom. Some builders may want to bevel the transom sides to allow the side planks to fit tight and flush. The bevel can be anywhere from 10 to 20 degrees, depending on the length and width of the skiff; fifteen degrees is average. You can use a saw, hand plane, or wood rasp to shape the bevel, or simply omit the bevel.

the transom to the front of the boat with a measuring tape or piece of string; the distance should be the same or very close. If it is not, go back and check your work, because something is out of alignment. The good thing about bedding compound is that it can be disassembled easily, because it is not an adhesive. If everything is in alignment, continue with the assembly. If it is just a little out of alignment and you can't find the problem, forget about it; it will not be noticed when the boat is completed.

At this point, fasten the planks to the

transom with two screws on each side; this will hold everything tight so you can inspect your work again. You can use nails, but they are more difficult to remove if you need to make adjustments.

Place the remaining fasteners about 2 inches apart and tighten everything up. To complete this assembly, use screws or nails, taking time to drill pilot holes to prevent splitting the plank ends.

If you view the transom from the top, looking straight down where the side planks join the right and left transom edges, you will see a V-shaped gap. Some boat builders remove this gap by cutting a matching angle on the transom sides of about 15 degrees before assembly. If you have the capability to do this, fine; if not, don't worry about it, because most of the old skiff builders only had a few hand tools and they just caulked these gaps with bedding compound and a dab of paint.

Top down view of a construction model showing the completed transom with an outboard motor cutout. Note the rear seats, transom corner braces, and double gunwale arrangement.

Remove the Spanish Windlass and clean up any bedding compound that has oozed out of your joints. Now inspect your project. Do not trim the planks flush with the transom at this time. After the top planks are in place, everything can be trimmed flush.

When working alone or with solid wood planks a Spanish Windlass can be used to bend the planks into shape and hold them while positioning the transom for fastening. A short stick is placed in the rope loop and twisted to bring the planks together. *Photo by Mark Freeland*

Step 5: Installing the Stem

At this point, the front of the boat is being held together by the small piece of soup can sheet metal. The actual stem piece needs to be shaped and installed permanently. Place the boat structure on top of your two low work benches if it is not already on them, and then place the front of the boat so the stem wood rests flush on the bench. Place the 2×4 stem wood into the V created by the sheet metal and two planks.

Look at it. The stem wood can be turned in two directions depending on the style you want. One way is with the narrow face of the 2×4 facing forward, and the other way is with the wider side facing forward. Both will work well. Keep in mind that a dressed 2×4 today is actually 1½ inches thick and 3½ inches wide. With the wide face of your stem wood facing forward, you will have more material available

to accept fasteners. This will create a blunt bow, but this look can be offset with the addition of a false stem. The blunt bow shape was popular years ago because it was easier to construct with hand tools and install with nails than a narrow stem. Both styles are really pretty easy to do. With this skiff example, we will use the wide face of the 2×4 forward. I know cutting angles is bothersome and for many first timers making any kind of mistake is terrifying. Most builders now use a table saw or band saw for cutting stem angles. Making these cuts with hand tools is easy, too.

With your stem piece 2×4 in place, determine the angle to be cut. You can use a ruler or an angle gauge. I usually set the 2×4 on top of the lower planks where the planks come together, eyeballing the placement. Reaching under the 2×4 on the end where it is sitting on top of the planks, trace the angle on the end of the stem wood. Turn it over to get the other end and make sure you've kept the correct end forward. Now lay out the sides of the stem with a straight edge and connect the lines. Darken this small area of wood to be removed with your pencil so it is easy to see. Remove the wood outside of the markings with a handsaw or just use a plane. If you use a hand plane you will remove the wood a little at a time with less chance of taking off too much. Try the fit, and if more wood needs to be removed, use the plane again or a wood rasp like those big horse hoof files.

The next step is to fasten the stem to the lower planks. You have several choices at this point. You can spread glue on the stem piece, or use bedding compound. Before good-quality water-resistant adhesives became available, bedding compounds like Dolifinte were the preferred choice for wood-to-wood joints. With bedding compound you get a good waterproof seal, and if you need to remove the stem in the future, you can disassemble the wood parts without destroying everything. That's not always true when using glue. I use bedding compound with mechanical fastening and use glue on a few components where the extra strength it provides is an advantage to the overall construction.

After the spreader stick and transom is in place, use a bevel gauge to determine the stem angle. *Photo by Mark Fleetwood.*

If you do not have a bevel gage, a simple method for taking off the stem angle is to place a piece of paper or scrap wood under the stem area and trace it with a pencil. This becomes a pattern for the stem angle. *Photo by Mark Freeland*

As with the transom, drill pilot holes for the screws or nails about 2 inches apart to prevent end-grain splitting. After the planks are fastened, wipe off excess goop. Today's water soluble glues can be cleaned off easily with warm water before they set, but are almost impossible to remove after they dry. Oil-based bedding compounds can be removed with a little mineral spirits. After this is done, remove the metal soup can and save it for your next boat or recycle.

Do not trim the lower planks flush with the stem at this time, and do not cut the stem to make it shorter. This will be done when we fit the false stem and add the deck. Stand back and look at what you have accomplished. Your project should have a boat shape. This is a good time to take a break and check things; when building boats, always do your best to stop when you have equal symmetry. Use your tape measure and string to make sure of the symmetry. If you are off a bit, don't worry about it. Never stop when you have two planks on a side and one on the other. Something might come up that would prevent you from getting back to the project for a while, and leaving the boat in this situation can stress the hull shape. Remember we are building this boat without building a frame or jig. Our boat is the building frame.

Step 6: Installing Inside Stringers

The next thing we do is strengthen the bottom side planks by adding stringers, because they string from the front to the back. These also provide material for nailing into when we add the next layer of planks and the bottom. These stringers act as doublers. When wood was a full dimension from the lumber yard, you didn't need to do this. But with the dressed stock we have today, it makes for a stronger boat to add these stringers. For stringers you can use any 1×2-inch stock. Cut and trim it to fit inside the two planks you have just installed, on the inside top and on the inside bottom. Attach the long stringers with PVA glue and nail to the planks lengthwise. I use small #6 nails. Clean off the excess PVA glue with a rag and warm water before it sets. You may need to go over it several times to get all of the glue drips. PVA glue sets up hard and can prevent stain penetration. If you are planning to use a stain or natural finish, dried glue can seal the wood surface and create a blotchy look.

Don't worry if a few of your #6 1¼-inch nails protrude on the other side of the bottom planks. They can be nipped or filed off or covered by the top planks. Some stores do not carry 1¼-inch hot-dipped galvanized nails, so I use 1½-inch nails, or whatever I can get, and drive them in at angle so they do not go through the lower planks.

Step 7: Installing the Top Planks

Attaching the top planks is similar to attaching the bottom planks, but just enough different to be confusing. I find the top planks easier to do because our boat structure is now more rigid and up off the ground on our benches. Our top planks are plywood and have been joined using butt blocks. You could use solid plank material for the top strakes; however, our example uses ply. The ply bends easy and, unlike like the bottom plank assembly, you can bend one side at a time now because the hull is rigid.

To make the upper planks lay flat to the lower planks at the stem and transom, you will need to cut spacers; these spacers allow the planks to lap correctly. If your lower planks were made from solid plank wood ¾-inch thick, you can use this material; however, the solid wood spacers have a tendency to split, so drill pilot holes. You can also laminate two pieces of ⅜-inch marine ply together to make your spacers, or if you still have some, use your leftover ¾-inch plywood from the transom construction. The spacers need to be only about 3 inches wide and are placed above, and resting on, the top of the lower planks at the stem and transom. We do not want any gaps to allow water intrusion later. Make them about 1 foot long for now and trim them at the top later.

I used to glue the side planks together, but it makes such a mess. Caulk them later when the boat is upside-down. If you have someone to help you here, it makes the job easier, but you can do it by yourself. Position the upper plank on the stem, use bedding compound or glue, and lap it over the bottom plank two inches, observing how it needs to go together. Mark it with your pencil. I use one nail or screw to hold the plank in position, and then position the middle of the plank so the lap is correct at the butt block and fasten it, and lastly bend the plank to the transom. If everything fits correctly, go back and place fasteners into the stem to make the bow joint stronger and then work your way back toward the transom, placing fasteners every 6 inches or so. Fill in the middles later, and when completed you will have fasteners about every 3 inches. If you wish, place fasteners every two inches for a stronger joint.

Spread bedding compound or glue on the transom sides and attach the top plank to the transom with screws or nails after drilling pilot holes. Do the opposite side the same, making sure the laps meet at the stem and transom. Look at the front and back of the boat; the laps should be in the same place and look even. If

Before adding the upper planks, spacers must be added to the stem and transom sides so the planks lay flush above the lower planks. There are several methods for doing this; however, this is the simplest. *Photo by Mark Freeland*

The second row of planks is being added to the Thoreau boat. There will be a total of two planks to each side with this boat. The planking is beveled cedar clapboard siding. Because of the bevel, two small pieces of siding are used for each spacer. This makes each beveled plank lay flat to the next. *Photo by Mark Freeland*

Fastening planks on the other side of the Thoreau boat. Never leave your boat project with unequal symmetry, because these boats are not built on a building frame. The hull structure is the frame. *Photo by Mark Freeland*

Drilling pilot holes with the push drill. Nails are used to hold the planks together and fasten the second row of planks to the lower planks. Later the nails will be bent over against the inside stringers and clenched tight to hold the planks. *Photo by Mark Freeland*

A cedar plank is ripped for trim, spacers, and small braces. Use all available wood to reduce waste. *Photo by Mark Freeland*

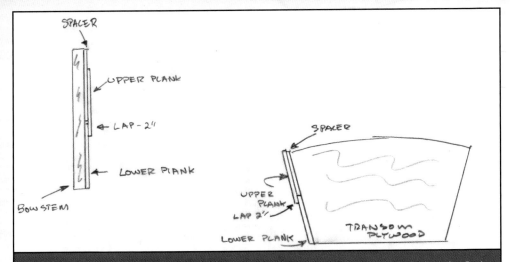

This sketch shows the relationship of the planks to the spacers, allowing the upper planks to lay flush on the bottom planks.

you have made a mistake, it can be corrected by repositioning the plank or trimming it with a plane. Don't worry if the front and back of the boat is a little off. Now trim the excess wood that is hanging past the transom. Trim it flush, and caulk any gaps later. The stem will be trimmed after the deck installation.

Clean up any excess glue or bedding compound and sand the inside of the boat structure with medium and then fine sandpaper.

On the Thoreau boat, stringers are being fastened to the second row of planks for strength. The cedar bevel siding is thinner on one side and requires reinforcement. *Photo by Mark Freeland*

The combination boat model showing two planks to a side, deck, daggerboard, and cut out transom for a small outboard motor. The finish is natural with a rubbed oil mixture of pine tar, linseed oil, and gum turpentine. This finish is often called a Down East mix. *Photo by Mark Freeland*

Two construction models shown together for comparison. The boat in the foreground is a rowboat. Note its narrow width, raked transom, and sleek lines. *Photo by Mark Freeland*

Sometimes it is difficult to force stringers to make a tight bend without deforming thin planks. Cedar planking is ripped to make thin strips of wood for laminated stringers. *Photo by Mark Freeland*

A hoof knife, or crooked knife, is used to remove excess dried glue. *Photo by Mark Freeland*

Trim the plank ends flush with the transom. *Photo by Mark Freeland*

Adding a second row of planks to the transom and fastening them with nails. *Photo by Mark Freeland*

The boat is upside-down on two benches. Nails are clenched with two hammers. The heavier hammer is placed against the nail head and the smaller hammer bends the nail into the wood. Holding a heavy hammer to the nail head is called bucking. *Photo by Mark Freeland*

With the boat upside-down, plane the transom and plank edges flat for a tight seal when the bottom plywood is installed. *Photo by Mark Freeland*

The bottom stringers at the bow are clenched where there is little room to work. A crack on the second row of planks is repaired by splicing in another piece of cedar and gluing it into place. *Photo by Mark Freeland*

A block plane is used to smooth the deck trim. The side planking has not been caulked. *Photo by Mark Freeland*

The boat has now been caulked with a thick mixture of pine tar and fine sawdust. The false stem is in place. The pine tar will take a few weeks to dry. *Photo by Mark Freeland*

A small deck ties the upper bow structure together. With the addition of the bottom planking, the front of the boat becomes a rigid assembly. *Photo by Mark Freeland*

Aft view looking forward. The boat is ready for bottom planking. Note how the stem with the spreader stick and angled transom form the hull shape by twisting the planks and creating flare. *Photo by Mark Freeland*

View of the spreader stick and stringers. The hull planks are nailed through the reinforcing stringers and clenched over. A spacer block is in position for row locks. *Photo by Mark Freeland*

Step 8: Planking the Bottom

This is a major step in the boat construction, but it is easy. When putting on the skiff bottom, even if you are going to use plywood for the bottom instead of traditional solid wood planks, the task is called planking the bottom. Turn the boat over and look at the bottom edges of the hull. See how the curve of the hull, along with the twist of the planks into the transom, has created flare on the hull planks. As I have said, flare is an important design element. Flare (wider at the top than bottom) adds volume and weight-carrying capacity. In the days of the working skiffs, watermen might load 1,000 pounds of cargo and the gunwale might come to within inches of the water. A safe limit today would be three people, about

The boat is upside-down and ready for the bottom planking. Plywood for the bottom is in place and marked to shape for cutting. *Photo by Mark Freeland*

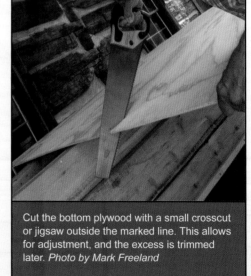

Cut the bottom plywood with a small crosscut or jigsaw outside the marked line. This allows for adjustment, and the excess is trimmed later. *Photo by Mark Freeland*

Fit the bottom planking into place before fastening; always mark the plywood panels to make sure they return to the same position. *Photo by Mark Freeland*

Spread bedding compound or glue on the hull plank edges and the bottom 2×4 spreader stick/butt block. Because it is the largest panel, the aft plywood bottom panel is positioned for fastening first. *Photo by Mark Freeland*

The aft bottom panel is in place and fastened so it will not move. Bedding compound or glue is spread on the forward half of the bottom spreader stick/butt block and plank edges. Another short piece of 2×4 was added from the bottom spreader stick forward to the stem. This ensures a strong bow structure. *Photo by Mark Freeland.*

600 pounds for a 12-foot boat. Also notice how the planks are bent outward by the spreader stick, and the bottom of the hull has formed a curve from front to back. This is called rocker.

Lay one of the 1×2 sticks across the hull bottom with the stick on edge. Notice that the hull edge is not flat in relation to the stick, because of the twist in the side planks. These edges must be made flat and square to the bottom so the plywood will fit flat when caulked and fastened down. It must be as flat as you can make it to prevent water leaks. Plane until there is no light showing under the stick. Take your time and don't get over-zealous with the plane.

The next step is to make a combination spreader stick and butt block for the bottom of the boat, using a 2×4. This will be installed approximately under your spreader stick that is now attached to your hull. This new spreader will first be fastened to the lower side planks and then to the plywood bottom. Measure from the transom forward 8 feet, the length of a sheet of your bottom plywood, and position the bottom spreader so both the rear and the forward sheet of plywood can share the 2×4. Fit the 2×4 flush and across the boat bottom. Make sure the wide side of the 2×4 is facing up; this will provide more surface to fasten the plywood bottom. Eyeball the angle or use an

angle gauge and cut it to fit. Most of the time these angles are about 5 to 10 degrees.

Spread bedding compound on each end of the 2×4 and attach it with two long nails or screws on each side. Note how the fasteners and 2×4 ties the boat hull together at the bottom, adding strength. Unlike the upper spreader stick, the lower one will be on the bottom, so bedding compound is required to prevent water from seeping through any small cracks. The bottom spreader stick serves a dual purpose. It becomes the butt block to join the two bottom plywood pieces end to end as well as reinforce the two bottom planks side to side.

Next, lay two of the sheets of the bottom

Nail the bottom down with aluminum ring-shank vinyl siding nails. The large heads work well with plywood by spreading the load to prevent tear-out. *Photo by Mark Freeland*

Hammer the nails in from the side plank edges and at a slight angle so the nails conform to the hull flare. Photo by Mark Freeland

plywood on the boat and dry-fit them. If you wish, get someone to help you wrestle the plywood into place, or put weights on the plywood pieces to hold them down and keep them from moving while you take a pencil and draw around the boat several times, marking the ply for cutting, and marking left and right, front and back to prevent errors. Your boat will probably not be perfect on each side, but that will not hurt the performance. After the panels are removed, cut them a bit outside the line. You can plane or sand the edge smooth later once the bottom is installed. You should have enough plywood left over for the deck and the transom corner braces.

When you have cut out the bottom pieces, fit them into place, making sure everything is the way you want it. If you didn't mark them, do it now. Also mark a line all the way around the boat on the outside of the plywood where you will place your nails, about ⅝ of an inch from the outside edge. This line is a guide for placing your bottom rails, so that they go into the planking evenly. You don't want any nails coming through the sides of your boat hull. When you hammer them in make sure they go in at a slight angle to match the hull flare angle. I usually hammer nails 6 to 8 inches apart first to get the bottom on quickly, and then nail in the middles. This places the fasteners every 3 inches or so.

Bedding compound is a good material for wood joints because it never really dries out and remains pliable. It comes in white, gray, and mahogany. Some builders prefer to use polyurethane construction glue, which is available at home center stores. It comes in caulking tubes and is applied with a caulking gun. It is highly water resistant and will fill gaps. I have used this material myself; however, once it sets up, making adjustments or repairs is difficult.

You can attach the bottom by yourself, but it is easier with a helper. I prefer to use aluminum ring shank, vinyl siding nails. They look like roofing nails and will not back out, nor will they corrode much. You can also use stainless ring shank nails. However, not all stainless is created equal. The stainless alloy for nails should be 316, but many of these fasteners are made from 304, which is not as corrosion resistant. Below the waterline, lower-quality stainless alloys can corrode in saltwater from oxygen starvation. With small skiffs like these, it isn't as much of a problem as it is with larger craft. You can even use the plain galvanized nails you have used for everything else if you wish. I like the aluminum nails because they have large heads and ringed shanks. These two qualities hold the plywood bottoms on tightly, preventing separation of the ply from the soft pine lower planks and stringers.

Excess bedding compound will ooze out of your joints. Clean everything now, after the bottom is attached. Next, turn the boat right side up and clean the inside, too. Where the compound has oozed out of the joints, use a little mineral spirits on your gloved finger to wipe a nice smooth fillet. When its surface dries and skins over in a few days, everything can be painted over. If you are going for a natural finish, use mahogany-colored bedding compound. If I am painting, I use the white or gray compound because sometimes the mahogany color will bleed through light paint colors. If you are going to use acrylic paints, use oil-based wood primer for the inside and outside of the boat. The oil-based primer soaks into the wood and seals the oil-based bedding compound and prevents it from bleeding through. When you have finished cleaning the inside, turn the boat over again with the bottom facing up.

Step 9: Installing the Rub Strip and Skeg

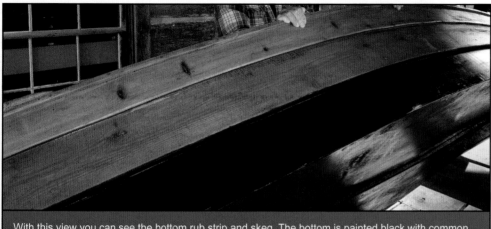

With this view you can see the bottom rub strip and skeg. The bottom is painted black with common oil-based exterior enamel. The top sides are finished with a Down East mix of several coats and then buffed with a soft cloth. *Photo by Mark Freeland*

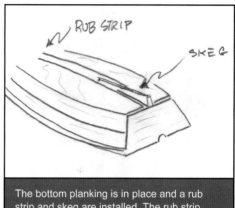

The bottom planking is in place and a rub strip and skeg are installed. The rub strip provides protection for the bottom and controls bottom flexing. The skeg helps the boat track straight in the water when rowing, motoring, or sailing.

These are optional, but I always install them on my skiffs. The rub strip also strengthens the bottom. It is a common 2×4 long enough to cover the bottom. A 2×4 12 feet in length will work well. Lay a 12-foot 2×4 flat on the bottom of the boat, starting at the stern, and flush with the outside of the transom. Mark it with a pencil so it is in the middle of the boat. Spread bedding compound on the 2×4 and place it into your marked position. Drill pilot holes in the end next to the transom and fasten it with two screws side by side. Make sure the screws go into the bottom transom brace. This will anchor the rear portion of the strip into a frame.

Anchor the 2×4 to the bottom butt block that crosses the boat in the middle with two screws as before. This, too, anchors the rub strip into a frame. Then anchor the forward end into the stem wood with two screws. Some 2×4 material will need to be trimmed off the front of the boat, but not right now.

Turn the boat over, and using screws or aluminum ring shank nails, fasten from the inside through the ⅜-inch bottom plywood and into the 2×4. This makes for a very tight joint. I usually do this with a zigzag pattern every 4 inches. Remember to wipe off the excess bedding compound on the bottom of the boat. I always try to work as neatly as possible, cleaning up as I go along.

Attach the skeg in a similar fashion. Mount it from the inside with screws. It is nothing more than a 2×4 on edge cut into a triangle shape about 14 to 18 inches in length. Shape it a little with a file and sandpaper if you wish. I like to make them replaceable, because they do take a beating. Use plenty of bedding compound for any part that is attached to the bottom and under the water.

Step 10: Installing a False Stem

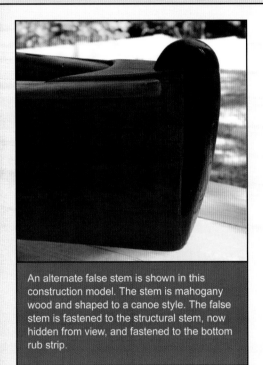

An alternate false stem is shown in this construction model. The stem is mahogany wood and shaped to a canoe style. The false stem is fastened to the structural stem, now hidden from view, and fastened to the bottom rub strip.

I often install a false stem. The false stem covers up the plank ends and makes a watertight seal when caulked. Use plenty of bedding compound here and never glue, because you might need to remove it in the future. A false stem absorbs shock and takes wear. Even though I don't mean to hit the dock or pier, I do sometimes. On my work skiffs I cut a piece of old tire and screw it to the false stem. Then if I hit something, I am prepared. The impact is quieter, too.

Sometimes I cut false stems with a slight curve to give the skiffs a canoe bow. The canoe bow, and the gentle curve of the sheer with a slightly raked stern, provide a more fluid look than the standard boxy flatiron skiffs. If you are not sure, make a few cardboard templates and pick the one you like the best.

Trace the false stem pattern on a piece of 2×4 or other lumber and cut it to shape. Then take a good look at the front of your boat. When you installed the 2×4 rub strip on the bottom, there should be a little piece protruding out the front. Your false stem will rest on top of this and will be fastened with two screws through the bottom rub strip and into the false stem, as well as other screws into the stem frame. Use plenty of bedding compound and attach it to the frame stem with screws. Trim the false stem and frame stem at the top later.

Now is the time to drill a hole for your bow eye and install it. This is easiest to do now, while you have room to work. If you forget, it is all right. It will only be slightly more difficult to work under the deck. I like to use quality forged, hot-dipped galvanized bow eyes from the hardware or farm store. The fancy ones at the marine store are fine, but they look out of place on these boats, and they carry a marine price tag, too. Get one large enough for a good-size rope and make sure the shank is long enough to go through the false stem and frame stem. If you are going to hang a piece of tire on the stem, get a big washer for under the bow eye so it does not go through the rubber tire, and one for the back to protect the stem wood, along with a lock washer and then the nut. I usually place these bow eyes one-third of the way up from the bottom of the stem. If you ever need to tow this boat in the water behind a larger craft, having the bow eye low lifts the bow up and out of the water for better towing and the skeg keeps the boat going straight. These little things can be adjusted to suit your specific requirements.

Step 11: Installing the Seats

You can design your seats any way you want. They can be made from 1×12s with some bracing added underneath for strength. You can even use plywood. Thin plywood will need a fair amount of bracing and thicker ply not so much. In the example we are going to use the same 1×12 solid wood we used for our lower planks.

Begin with the middle seat. It is located on top of the upper spreader stick, and the spreader stick now becomes a seat brace. Measure and fit a 1×12 to size. Sometimes I use two 1×10

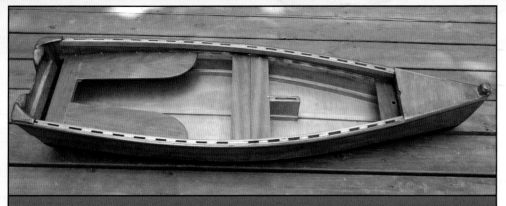

A construction model shows a seat arrangement for a 16-foot combination boat. The curved back seat arrangement allows plenty of room for operating an outboard motor or managing a tiller for a rudder.

Another example of a rear seat on a 16-foot rowboat, with the seat supported by the side plank stringers, a transom brace, and a brace under the seat, not shown. This skiff is made from pine planking to replicate a nineteenth-century pulling boat.

Another view of seat examples; note the hardwood row locks. These are designed to slip into the gunwale spaces so rowing positions can be changed from the middle to forward seats. This was once a common arrangement, with the fishing guide in front and the sport casting a line in the back.

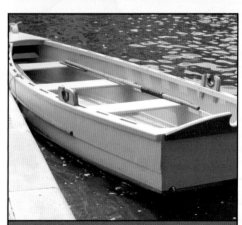

A 16-foot flatiron skiff on the Indianapolis, Indiana, Central Canal with the three forward seats in view. The rear seat is not shown. This is now a rental boat.

planks together for wider seats. When measuring, consider the slight curve of the hull planks, and remember that you can always cut a little at a time until the seat fits perfectly. The seats will rest on the upper stringers of the lower planks and increase the overall strength of the boat. They are important structural members that make the hull more rigid.

Screw the seat edges into the stringers on each side of the boat and fasten three or four screws to the spreader stick as well. You can

A 12-foot construction model with a three-seat arrangement. Note how the middle seat with the spreader stick underneath defines the hull width and form. If you were to extend the hull lines rearward until they meet, you would have a good example of a fish form.

Cutting the rear seat curve for the Thoreau boat. *Photo by Mark Freeland*

Making seats for the Thoreau boat with pine wood and a small crosscut saw. *Photo by Mark Fleetwood.*

Drawing a seat curve with a folding rule used as a limber batten. Many boat builders prefer a wood folding rule because it is perfect for tracing a quick curve to remove the boxy look from flatiron skiffs. *Photo by Mark Fleetwood.*

Cutting a front seat curve for the Thoreau replica. *Photo by Mark Freeland*

The completed Thoreau boat. The replica is in spirit only; no one really knows what it looked like. The replica illustrates the common flatiron skiff construction methods used throughout this book. *Photo by Mark Freeland*

nail the seats in place, but it will be difficult to remove them if you need to get under a seat for a future repair.

Next fit the bow seat. In a 12-foot boat, it will be about 3 feet back from the stem and made and fastened the same way as the middle seat. If you are going to use the front seat as a mast support for sailing, make it strong with two 2×4 or 2×2 braces. For a 12-foot boat, 2×2 front seat braces are more than adequate. As you can see, the seats tie the boat halves together.

Install the rear seat last. The back of the rear seat should be about 6 inches forward from the transom. This will give you enough room to get your hands behind the seat to clean out debris. I always make rear seats double or triple wide so you can sit sideways to operate an outboard motor or sailboat tiller. As a general rule, use 2×4 braces for the rear seat; however, 2×2 braces are adequate for a 12-foot boat.

I often make a curved stern seat to break up the boxy design and make it more comfortable. I always take the opportunity to add curves whenever possible. If I make a curved rear seat I always add a slight curve to the back of the front seat, too.

Step 12: Installing Spacer Blocks, Inside and Outside Gunwales

Gunwale is an old word pronounced "gunnel" and was originally made very strong to support a swivel cannon on the "captain's gig," a boat used for transportation from ship to ship or ship to shore. Gunwales provide strength and stiffen the hull's upper planks where they wear. Here we will use a double gunwale.

Before you add the spacer blocks and inside gunwales, you need to determine where the row locks will be positioned. The easiest way to do this is to sit on the middle seat with your arms stretched out as if you are about to make the pull stroke—arms straight out in front of your chest. Mark on either side of the boat the length from the middle of the seat to your hands as if they were gripping oars. Ask someone to help you measure and make sure the distance is the same on both sides of the boat. You may discover the butt blocks used to join the upper planks are in the correct position or close to it. If so, these will become the mounts for the row locks. If not, cut two 6-inch blocks from your 1×2 stock, and glue and nail them on the mark. Put the mark in the middle of the blocks. When you get ready to fasten the oar locks to the blocks, you will have enough room to make final adjustments. If the butt blocks extend above the sheer line, trim them flush.

The next step is to cut 4-inch blocks from the same 1×2 stock and measure from the row lock blocks outward to both ends of the boat. Skip every other one and count how many blocks you will need. Why the spaces? For one thing, when you tip your boat on its side, this lets the water run out. Those spaces also make handy places to tie off an anchor or minnow bucket or tie up to the dock. Use glue and then nail all of the blocks into position. These blocks should be short enough to manage the hull curve. Use longer blocks for a longer boat, and 4-inch blocks for a shorter boat. You might need to sand or plane a little material away to make a snug fit and follow the hull curve. If you forget to do that, the gaps can be filled with putty later.

If you are going to paint or stain the blocks the same as the inside of the hull, it is best to do it now, before you put inside trim on the wood blocks. I often forget to do this and then have to spend time with a small paint brush, and I always miss areas. When the boat is almost finished you can install the inside trim. It is easier to paint this trim now before it is installed and then do a little touch-up later.

Install the outer gunwales. These rails were often made from oak or some other tough hardwood and left natural. You can use hardwood or the 1×2 pine trim stock. If you use pine, it is best to paint it, as it is soft and easily damaged.

Install the outer gunwales with bedding compound and screws so it can be replaced later. Never glue outer gunwales. Hardwood gunwales left natural or painted in a contrasting color set off the sheer line—the hull edge curve at the top.

Step 13: Installing the Deck

If you plan to paint or finish the inside of your boat, it is easier to do it before you install the deck. There are many deck styles—be creative. A slight curve and camber to the deck sheds water and adds eye appeal. You can use your remaining plywood or the planks to build it if you wish. The deck adds strength, so if you go without one, at least make a little pie shaped piece up in front, as I did on the Thoreau replica.

In this case, I am using a piece of ⅜-inch marine plywood to make a sturdy, functional deck about 18 inches long, and with an arc to match the seat curve. Trace the bow shape on the plywood so it fits the front of the boat; I usually cut deck material a little oversized, and after it is installed, trim it to fit with a plane and then sand it smooth. Use bedding compound and fasten it with nails or screws. The deck, in conjunction with the attached plywood bottom, will tie the front of the skiff together. The structure will be very strong.

Now look at the false stem and the frame stem. The long frame stem can be cut to match the false stem at the top, and shaped with a wood rasp and sanded to a pleasing curve. A 4- to 6-inch stem above the deck will give your skiff a classic look and a handy place to tie off a line.

Step 14: Installing Corner Braces

The transom needs to be braced at the top corners to increase strength. This is very important if you plan on using an outboard motor. There are lots of ways to do this, and plywood cut into a pleasant curve works well and is strong. I always glue and nail the braces. If you use glue, leave the wood bare in this area to allow the glue to penetrate the wood fibers. After installation you can sand everything smooth and then apply the finish.

Step 15: Painting and Finishing

Historically, these are simple boats and a simple finish is best. Low-sheen and semi-gloss paints diminish surface blemishes. Plywood surfaces, especially end grains, need to be sealed. As I have said, I use varnish sparingly and prefer the softer oil finishes that can be refreshed throughout the season by wiping them with an oil-soaked cloth.

When painting or varnishing, several thin coats are better than heavy ones. Finishing this way prevents drips and unsightly sags. Try to start painting in the morning, and on low-humidity days. Watch the weather forecast, too. You want your paint to be dry to the touch before evening dust begins to settle.

At this point your basic skiff is finished. Chapter 3 covers oars and oar locks and skiff variations, so take a break, you deserve it. While you are thinking about all those little things that need to be done before getting your boat wet, the following true skiff tale will get your imagination working.

When Starlight Danced a Tango

It was the last day of the Small Craft Festival at Mystic Seaport in Connecticut, and I sat with my back against an old pie safe in a coffee shop way down at the end of the road by the drawbridge. Yarn after yarn eased the time along, and so it went into the evening. Most of the tourist crowd had left and the owner, himself an old salt, quietly walked around pulling the shades down and locked the door. Maybe there were ten of us left, some locals and my crew from the boat show. The owner made an announcement that we could hang around awhile, but the coffee shop was officially closed, and if anyone wanted a refill he would be happy to oblige with an added tot of rum or whiskey for the same price as a plain coffee. Most everyone used the opportunity for a refill.

He and his brother had inherited this building from their parents. It had been a dry goods store, then a hardware store, and now this coffee shop. Years ago, the younger brother, Paul, had bought out his older brother Henry, who headed south where winters weren't so wintery. After we had settled in with our coffee of choice, Paul cut the lights a bit, and with a light rain working its magic on the old metal roof, looked around the room.

"I don't recognize any of you at the moment and all of you are younger than me, so I'll tell this tale and set the evening straight," he said.

Paul sat on a stool, sipped his coffee, and began.

The wind came across Fishers Island Sound as raw as the oysters Henry and his brother Paul had eaten for lunch. In another twenty minutes it would be completely dark and like all good fishermen, the boys sat quietly on the water and waited. They had fortified themselves against the October night with a half-dozen bacon sandwiches and a big thermos of coffee. For two nights straight, they had been out here in their father's big flatiron skiff. It was bigger than most of its type, over twenty feet on the water line and near eight feet in breadth. With a strong mast and a good sprit sail, a real iron-weighted centerboard, and a big rudder, the boat could handle most anything with a good crew. A culling board up front just behind the rowing seat with a well in the middle made it a fisherman's boat sound and true. Hand-painted block letters on the transom called out the skiff's name, *Starlight*. Henry told his brother that three times is a charm.

A German submarine had been spotted in the area, and everyone was alerted to watch for it and do their part. It was the time of their country and these boys weren't going to let an opportunity slip by. It was 1944. They had a couple hundred feet of cod line, a fish billy, and a desire to do the impossible.

Paul added a little bit more rum to his coffee and looked the crowd over. He had our attention.

"I truly believe there are times when you can will something to happen. I can't prove it, but I know it's true."

The coffee shop bunch was not talking. We were listening.

In the skiff and way off in the distance Henry could see lightning. He checked his pocket watch. Lightning wasn't uncommon in early October.

Paul Tucker shifted his weight on the stern seat and held the thermos. "You know, Henry, if we don't get back before nine, Mom is really going to get mad and we'll do more chores this weekend."

Under ordinary circumstances Paul would have followed his older brother into the gaping jaws of fear itself, but tonight this eight-year-old was just like any other person who would have been out here: cold, tired, and miserable.

Henry, on the other hand, carried optimism beyond faith. He saw the world with a clarity of vision that most people lose as soon as they reach adulthood. He pulled hard on the starboard oar and put the shadow of Fishers Island behind them. Henry spoke to his brother with the firm tone of command. "Be quiet and hand me another one of those sandwiches, and pour me a coffee too."

The night got darker and *Starlight* danced on the water. The wind and chop were increasing and the temperature had come up a bit. They were intent on staring into the void beyond their skiff. Then they heard it. At first the sound was like someone taking a deep breath, and then the water, not a hundred yards away moved with the ferocity of a gushing torrent. The black shape of a submarine, its pressure hull streaked with rust, lifted from the sea. The breathing sound became a roar, the air was filled with thick diesel fumes escaping from the ship's exhaust, and the smell of a hundred men living in precious little space rushed from the ventilators. The boys looked at each other in terror. The impossible had come, and it was as epic as the fear they felt. Tears dripped down Paul's face as he gripped the thermos with both hands.

Henry came alive like one being chased by demons. He stumbled to the front of the skiff and got the sail up in a series of quick jerks. He cut his hand on a splinter, wiped the blood on his shirt, and sighted up the mast. The canvas unfurled with a tug on the line, and a breeze caught the sail. Henry dropped the centerboard and told Paul to grab the tiller and steer straight ahead. With creaks and groans the skiff lurched after the submarine, and the brothers descended into a discussion of profound disagreement. The skiff ignored the heated words and name calling. It adjusted itself into an easy motion and took care of its occupants as it was built to do.

The night does not always give up its secrets, but tonight it did. As the Tucker boys sailed into the unknown, the submarine once again appeared in the blackness, this time moving in the opposite direction and heading out to sea. The wake from the big boat rocked the skiff and Henry tumbled face down over the middle seat. In that instant Paul looked up as the U-boat slipped by, illuminated in the feeble light. Almost within arm's reach, Paul saw a shape standing aft of the conning tower. Faint strains of a tango could be heard over the boat's loudspeakers. The shape turned and looked at Paul with pale eyes that had seen too much, revealing a man almost as young as his older brother. The shape waved, and Paul loosened his grip on the tiller and waved back. In the fleeting light, Paul saw the submariner smile, and the big boat disappeared into the night. Henry rolled over and sat back on the seat. He shouted orders like big brothers often do, but the fear that once held Paul in an iron grip was gone. He turned the skiff toward the island and Henry sheeted in the sail. The boys, cradled in the belly of a nice breeze, headed homeward with Henry nursing his hand and Paul steadfast at the tiller.

Some folks say a U-Boat could not have made it into the waters around Fishers Island. A good captain would not have chanced it, but others disagreed; the risk might have been worth it. The boys got home before nine, but they still received an extra load of chores for the weekend—not for being out late, but for spinning yarns. As for us, we made it back to our hotel, each one lost in thought, and the next day we headed in our own directions. On the drive home I thought about the previous week and the sailing yarn we had heard the night before. I decided I would always do my best to build strong boats with a will and purpose. There would be no other way.

3

Design and Material Variations

This part of the book is about variations on this model and other bits of information essential to wood boat building. Keep in mind that every design in this book can be built for a reasonable cost by purchasing supplies as you need them. Advice from the old timers who built these skiffs was to think hard before you spend your money, and make sure your purchase is worth it. The vow I made to myself to build boats strong, with a will and purpose, has nothing to do with spending a lot of money on exotic wood and marine hardware. Hand-fashioned hardwood cleats from discarded lumber and natural-fiber rope from the hardware store can still make a good boat. Keep the cost low and your enjoyment high.

Oars

A set of traditional thole pin oars and pin locks.

All of the design options in this book require a good set of oars. You can buy them if you wish; however, good oars are not cheap, and it is pointless to own cheap oars. You will never be satisfied with their performance. Traditionally, good oars are handcrafted from ash wood and a few other woods. If you have a sailboat or motor boat, and the wind or motor fails to cooperate, the old watermen would tell you to "get out the ash breeze and go to work"—the ash breeze being the power derived from pulling on the oars and the slight breeze against your back. Rowboats were often called pulling boats because you sit facing backwards and pull on the oars. Forward-facing rowing mechanisms are available, but we are not going to discuss them here. Their reversing hinge row locks are very expensive and cost more than the boat we are building.

There are many different oar designs. Each type accommodates specific regional preferences, and some are more difficult than others. The designs I prefer are simple.

Making Simple Oars

My favorite oar-making technique does not use common oar locks; instead, a pin is used as the fulcrum for the oar to pivot against. The design goes back to the Viking age. The pins are called "tholes," which in Old Norse means coming from a tree. The pins are made from hardwood dowels, or use discarded broom handles. I never throw away a broom or rake without saving the handle.

Begin making the oars from a 6-foot-long 2×6 piece of lumber. On one end of the 2×6 measure in 1½ inches and mark it, and do the same on the opposite side and on the other end. Use a straight edge to draw a line from this mark all the way to the opposite end of your 2×6. Saw on this line to make two triangle-shaped boards. These will be made into two oars. A ripsaw is best for cuts with the wood grain; however your crosscut saw will work, just be patient.

Make the hand grips next. Measure on the larger ends of your now-tapered boards inward 2½ inches on the straight side, and from that mark draw a straight line 8 inches long downward and then over to the angled side. Remove this material and shape the hand grip with a wood rasp and finish with sandpaper. I make my hand grips in an oval shape, but round is fine, too.

Next, make and attach the oar blades. These are made from two pieces of ⅜-inch plywood 4 inches wide by 16 inches in length or longer if you wish. Sometimes I just use whatever ply I have available at the time. Round the edges and sand the blades smooth. Attach the blades with screws to the thinner end of oars on the angled side. The slight angle will not make any difference in rowing performance, and fastening the blade on the angled side of your board positions the hand grips correctly for rowing. Don't glue the blades, just use bedding compound and screws so they can be replaced when they get beaten up.

Next, determine where to install the thole pin oar lock. These will go where you have marked for oar locks. If you have not marked for rowing locks, get into the boat with your oars and decide where the pins should go by bringing the grips together with a 10-inch gap between the grips. Now mark on the oar on the inward edge of your boat.

The double gunwale you have built will not be large or strong enough for a thole pin lock. There is an easy remedy: Cut two pieces of 2×4 into 8-inch lengths. Cut slight angles on each end of the 2×4 pieces to take away the rough look, and sand them smooth. In the middle of each piece on the narrow side, bore a hole through the 2×4 to fit your dowel. Cut two dowels approximately 10 inches in length and glue them into place with PVA glue. Gluing makes this assembly more rigid. These are now your thole pin oar locks. Make the thole pins from hardwood like oak or ash. Old broom and rake handles are usually pretty good hardwood. As you use the oars you can shorten the thole pin a bit. Until you get used to using this type of oar, leave the pin long for awhile. Some folks like to mount them on the outside of their boat, and some mount them inside.

This is why I want you to have at least a 10-inch gap between the oars when you are sitting in the middle seat and in the rowing position. This gap should accommodate your oars in any position you choose, outside or inside.

Depending on the width of your gunwale, you may need to add a filler piece of wood plywood behind the oar lock assembly, so it will be even with the top of the sheer. This area will wear down in time. In Ireland I have seen a piece of well-tanned and oiled leather with a hole in it and stretched over the thole pin. This protects the lock assembly from wear. The leather is tacked on with copper tacks and can be replaced. Mount the assembly with screws or bolts.

For the oars, if you use ¾-inch dowels for pins, bore a 1⅛-inch-diameter hole into the flat side and middle of your oar. Use a file and sandpaper to round out the hole. Tallow was often used to lubricate the pin and oar. Place the oars over the pins with the flat of the oar blades facing toward the rear of your boat. These are very sturdy oars. The heavier end of the oars next to the rower provides better balance. As you use them, you can make the blades on the oars narrower if you wish, and, as I said, you can also shorten your thole pins an inch or so. If the oars still feel a little bulky, make adjustments by planing off some wood here and there. After a while you will decide what you like the best.

More on Oarlocks and the Case for Wood Dowels

There are many different oarlock designs to choose from, and cost ranges from a few dollars to several hundred; the most expensive are polished bronze and cast in a historic pattern at a custom foundry. There are inexpensive alternatives. The cheap oarlocks that are designed to clamp on cheap oars are terrible. They are electro-galvanized and fail shortly after you buy them. I prefer the hot-dipped galvanized iron ones purchased from marine suppliers. They are inexpensive and last forever. I am currently using a pair I purchased from a marine junk shop twenty years ago. Each type of oarlock will require fitting to the oar. Oars that are not pinned in the oar lock will require leathering with buttons, or a hard rubber oar button, to keep the oars from slipping in the lock. Kits to do this can be purchased from marine suppliers. Check the resources page.

The thole pin type uses a pin made from a hardwood dowel, and sometimes stainless steel or bronze. I like these because they eliminate metal locks altogether. Dowels of all sizes come in handy when building boats. I use them for filling in holes I have drilled in the wrong place, or splicing together a piece of broken plank.

Unlike a metal fastener, a dowel can be trimmed and sanded to where it is almost invisible.

This is a good time to mention building the boat without metal fasteners. Wood pegs were used to hold boats together well before the age of metal-working, and in many parts of the world it is still a preferred construction method. In this method holes are bored where you would place a nail, screw, or bolt. Instead of a metal fastener, a hardwood peg, slightly larger than the hole, would then be driven in with a mallet and trimmed flush later. These wood nails that come from trees are called tree nails and shortened to the term trunnels. If you want to do this on your boat, make up about fifty to start. These are nice for installing the gunwales, because you can smooth the gunwales easily with a plane and not be concerned with nicking the blade on a nail or screw head. If you use a dark wood for the gunwales, light-colored pegs make a pretty contrast, or vice versa.

Periodically, if I want something mindless to do I will set up my chopping block and split out a couple hundred white oak trunnels. Without modern distractions like television and computers, folks would sit around and do handwork of all kinds and talk. Boat building was often a village affair. Making wood pegs was just another chore to be done if you were going to build a boat. These activities aren't much different than my cousins and me sitting around straightening nails on a piece of railroad iron.

I like the trunnels about 6 inches long and no smaller than $5/16$-inch at the head top. When you split them, most come out tapered; they do not need to be round. I drill a $1/4$-inch hole and drive them in. I use wood glue or pine tar, depending on the type of skiff I am building. If you are pegging lapped planks together, drive one all the way through both planks, and then, about 3 inches away, drive another one in from the opposite direction. This locks the planks together. Trim the trunnels with a sharp chisel or flush-cutting flexible saw. Many times trunnels were set into blind holes and wedged at the bottom and top. I know this sounds laborious, but these were large wood pegs for big boats and usually soaked in linseed oil and tar or animal fat to improve assembly and longevity.

Design Variations

There are hundreds of skiff designs. All share similar properties, but each is different depending on their region and use. The crabbing and oyster skiffs had a lower freeboard—the top planks were closer to the water than those on the lobster skiffs. This made it easier for the waterman to work the oyster tongs and crab traps. The larger lobster skiffs provided

The 12-foot Thoreau boat fits into the back of a full-size pickup truck. *Photo by Mark Freeland*

The 16-foot rowing boat is upside-down, and the bottom stringers are fitted to increase the plank thickness for the bottom hull fasteners. This boat will be traditionally cross planked with cedar wood on the bottom and caulked with pine tar. No plywood is used in the construction.

This example shows the stem, spreader stick, transom, and side planks assembled into a boat shape. Note the twist in the lower planks created by the spreader and transom. This flare will continue with the addition of the upper planks.

The skiff is upside-down with the side planks installed.

The skiff is right-side-up. Side planks are in place, along with the stringers, curved deck brace, and T-shaped stem with a heavy false stem to protect the boat on the Indianapolis, Indiana, Central Canal's concrete retaining walls.

The 16-foot replica of a nineteenth-century pulling boat is ready for launch.

An arched top deck is being constructed. Note the large false stem. This can be removed and replaced easily when damaged.

The pulling boat on the Indianapolis, Indiana, Central Canal ready for a fun day on the water.

This view shows the cedar cross planks in place. They have been cut to fit, numbered, and are ready for fastening and caulking with pine tar.

A 16-foot combination boat on the water at the city park in Franklin, Indiana. This skiff is much wider than the nineteenth-century pulling boat and has a large transom to support an outboard motor. Note the plywood corner braces on the transom.

Note the raked stern of the boat and almost plum false stem. This adds visual balance to the boxy traditional design. The Thoreau boat at Camp Atterbury, Edinburg, Indiana. *Photo by Mark Fleetwood.*

The Thoreau boat being rowed at Camp Atterbury, Edinburg, Indiana. *Photo by Mark Freeland*

The Thoreau boat on the water at Camp Atterbury Edinburg, Indiana. Note the thole pin oars and pin locks. *Photo by Mark Fleetwood.*

Bow view of the Thoreau boat. Note the broad bow created by a trimmed 2×6 for the structural stem. The narrow false stem changes the visual impression of the flat bow arrangement. The top of the false stem and deck are painted dark green to draw the eye away from the flat stem. *Photo by Mark Fleetwood.*

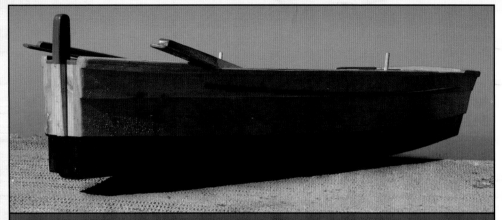

The Thoreau boat showing a traditional color scheme of the 1830s. The natural finish is the Down East mix, and the bottom is traditional oil-based black enamel. *Photo by Mark Freeland*

Example of a deck option on a rowing boat construction model. Curves reduce the flatiron skiff's boxy look.

Example of a large, flat plywood deck on a 16-foot construction model for a combination boat. The big deck controls spray when motoring or sailing. Note the notched deck to hold the mast in place after it goes through the seat notch.

Example of a large daggerboard box on a 14-foot construction model. The daggerboard has been removed so you can see how it is braced between the middle and front seat for strength.

Example of a daggerboard box on a fifteen-foot day boat with two masts. The box is mounted aft of the middle seat; the daggerboard is between the two sails, providing better rudder control by reducing weather helm. This 15-foot by 6-foot skiff performs like a bigger boat. It can easily seat six adults for a day of sailing.

On the day boat, the front seat and deck arrangement hold the foremast into position. The mast is laminated from four pine 1×4s and rounded with a plane. Masts and sails can be stored in the boat.

The day boat is on a trailer with sails up for adjustments. Both sails are lug-rigged, providing a total sail area of 110 square feet. The front sail is called the foresail on the foremast and the rear sail is called a mizzen on the mizzen mast. On small boats, the foresail is often called the main sail. This boat was shown at the 2011 Georgetown Wooden Boat Show, Georgetown, South Carolina.

The aft mizzen sail is smaller than the main; the mizzen mast is mounted off-center for tiller clearance and through the rear seat to a socket on the floor. The mizzen mast is laminated from two 1×4s cut with a rip saw and shaped with a plane.

An aft view of the day boat showing the transom and rudder arrangement. The rudder is laminated from three pieces of ½-inch plywood glued and nailed together with copper roofing nails. Edges are shaped and rounded to improve water flow across the rudder surface. The rudder is mounted to the transom with galvanized farm gate hardware.

A construction model of a 16-foot combination boat with a leg-o-mutton sail. This simple triangular sail, made from a painter's tarp, can be wrapped around the 12-foot mast and stored in the boat. The sail area on a full-size boat is approximately 50 square feet.

A construction model of a 14-foot combination boat rigged with a sprit sail and small jib. The sprit is the long, black pole supporting the end of the sail, and the jib is the small triangular sail in front. On a full size boat, the mast is about 10 feet tall, the sprit 12 feet long, and everything can be rolled up and stored in the boat.

A bottom view of the construction model for the 14-foot boat shows the skeg and bottom rub strip. The large daggerboard is in place. The daggerboard box is strongly built and retained to the boat's floor with large screws fastened through the bottom and into the frame of the box.

Rowing the 16-foot combination boat on the Indianapolis, Indiana, Central Canal. Note the movable hardwood oar locks and leathered oars. The oars are 8 feet in length providing a powerful stroke.

Rowing under a bridge with the silhouette of the boat and oars. Long oars are not practical in a crowded harbor. These long oars were replaced with shorter ones for rowing on the canal. When fishing guides once rowed their clients on big lakes and rivers, oars 12 feet or longer could be used for more power.

Wood thimbles and cleats made from scrap hardwood from a nearby cabinet shop. These thimbles work similar to a pulley and are made from white oak. The cleats are made from walnut and oiled with a Down East mix. All of these items are easy to make and cost virtually nothing except time.

The thimble round is first cut with a 2-inch hole saw and center bored with a ⅝-inch bit. The center hole is enlarged with a round file and sandpaper. The outside groove that holds the rope is made with a round file. The thimble is retained in a vice so that the ¼-inch manila rope can be wrapped with waxed twine.

A thimble at the head of a 12-foot mast is ready for the sail halyard to raise the sail. Thimbles can be made from any available hardwood. These items work well on small boats.

more room for bigger loads and a winch to aid in retrieving the heavy pots. Gunning skiffs were made low to the water so the hunters could sneak up on water fowl. Fishing skiffs were designed with a well for baskets covered in wet seaweed to keep the fish fresh. The sportsmen's boats had the rowing oars up front for the fishing guide, leaving plenty of room for the "sport" in back to cast his line. Each different skiff was altered slightly for specific purposes.

When building by eye you can make changes in your own boat to meet your own needs. You can't get into trouble with the small skiffs in this book. The designs are common and have been in use a long time. They are all suitable for protected waters and inshore use, provided the user is prudent. One would think that no one would ever overload a small boat beyond capacity and then head out into bad weather, but it does happen, and often. My advice is to take a safe boating class before going out. Most of these classes are free, except for a nominal charge for materials, and are sponsored by the United States Coast Guard and other organizations.

The next section covers several skiff variations: rowboat, motorboat, sailboat, a New England-style catboat skiff, and a scow skiff.

Improving the rowboat

If you are simply making a rowboat, there are a few minor deviations you can make from chapter 2 to improve the rowing capability. The boats we are building are narrower in respect to their length than boats of today; the main reason is that narrow boats go through the water with less resistance than wide boats. When the available power source is human or wind power, you want the design to be as efficient and as slippery through the water as possible. By shortening the spreader stick, increasing the twist in the planks by narrowing the transom dimensions, and increasing the transom rake, you can improve the rowing performance. By building a model of this variation, you can get a preview of what it will look like.

For example, build a model of the basic boat and then build a model of the improved rowing version and look them over. Pick the one you like best before cutting your wood. Do the same with the other versions. Building models in the winter when you can't get outside is time well spent. I cannot emphasize enough that model-building will make your project less frustrating. It also improves your building-by-eye skills.

Improving the motorboat

Because we are not building to a rigid set of plans, you can change a few things that allow the motorboat to carry more weight and use a more powerful motor. I have found the best size for a motor skiff is at least 16 feet long and 5 feet wide, with a transom width of 4 feet measured at the top of the transom. Once again, make a model and see what it will look like. You can add a little cuddy cabin up front to control spray, or install a portable potty, etc.

When I increase the size of a skiff beyond 16 feet, I add a third strake to the hull to make a greater depth within the boat. Build this boat as before by adding another plank, and then cut the shear curve on the uppermost planks. This makes a nice boat for rougher water and big enough to add the little cuddy cabin.

This is a good time to discuss outboard motors. When these boats first started using motors on their transoms, the motors were heavy in proportion to the horsepower they delivered. They were temperamental, noisy, and not fuel-efficient. Today's motors are lightweight, deliver adequate power for their size, and are very fuel efficient. I prefer small motors on these boats, because they can easily be overpowered. A ten-horsepower motor is more than adequate for a 16-foot boat. I have a six-horsepower motor that will push my larger skiff along just fine at half throttle. Of course, if you have a really big skiff it will require a larger motor and more hull strength to manage the increased stress, increasing the cost. Look at it this way: small boat, small cost.

Making a sailing skiff

This is the most complicated and expensive of all the design variations, because the sailing version requires several more unique pieces than the rowboat or motorboat. You can incorporate the sailing version into the basic rowboat and powerboat. In that way you would have a "three in one boat," which I call the combination boat. The overall performance will be acceptable. I find that the best sailing version of the skiffs we have discussed is the rowboat with an added sail rig, but it really doesn't matter. These aren't racing boats. When every option is a compromise, you give up something. It is the same with boats.

The sailing skiff will require a strengthened front seat to support a mast. You will need to add a daggerboard box and cut a slot in the bottom of the boat for the daggerboard to pass through. You will need to fashion a rudder and tiller so the boat can be steered, and mount it to the transom, and you will need to make the mast, boom, and other spars. Lastly, you will need an appropriate sail and rigging for it. I know this looks like a lot of extra stuff, but the good news is that you can always add the sailing rig later.

For my own boats I have two sail rigs, one small with a 45-square-foot lug sail, and one larger with a 60-square-foot lug sail. The lug sail design is very old and pretty close to a square sail. Everything rolls up on the mast and is secured with a couple of cords. These two sails will work for any 12-foot or 16-foot skiff, respectively, and can be stowed in the boat. The sails were purchased from a sail supplier and sized for simple boats of this type. The material is polyester sail cloth. I take my skiffs to wooden boat shows and I wanted nice-looking sails. The sails are red tanbark, which is a traditional color.

The biggest expense for the sailing rig is the sail. A custom sail will cost about what you have spent on the entire boat and maybe more if you want a specific color. There are ways around this, though. You can find a small used sail, or you can cut down an old sail and sew it yourself, make a new one from a sail kit, or make one over the weekend with common contractor's house wrap. House wrap is very tough, makes a decent sail, and instead of sewing you can use the special tape that comes with it. After several seasons using this sail, you can always decide to get one custom made. There are several types of house wraps available. They are usually made from synthetic material like polypropylene or polyethylene fibers. A special tape with an acrylic adhesive is sold along with the wrap, or you can sew it if you wish. I like this stuff, because you can make several types of sails and try them out on your boat. For example, you can make a sprit rig, a lug sail, or a leg-o-mutton, to name a few, and you haven't spent a fortune. Some builders special order house wrap with their company name printed on it. Ask around and tell them what you are doing, and they may donate some leftover material for your project—it's free advertising for them.

Effective sail sizes

Most of these skiffs had very simple sail rigs with small sails. The masts were fairly short, and unstayed, so the sails could be wrapped around them when not needed and stored in the boat. Some skiffs even used one of the oars for a mast and the other oar as a rudder. This kept equipment to a minimum. Big sails provide more power, but when the wind increases, they are hard to control on little boats with low freeboard. In the past, these skiffs might be loaded down with oysters, fish, and other cargo, and the skipper would not want to risk turning over and losing his load in high winds. Many of these watermen never learned how to swim either, and none worked with personal flotation devices back then.

For our skiffs, a sail area of 45 to 75 square feet is adequate. I know there are many one-design racing sailboats of that size that have twice or three times that sail area, but these skiffs were never designed to be sailed in that fashion on a daily basis. Their sails were always on the conservative side. Getting back to port and selling your catch was more important than racing. However, occasionally these boats would race each other; the bigger sails would come out and the skipper and crew would do their best to beat their opponents. For everyday working, smaller sails were the norm.

Several years ago while working on the Isle of Mann, I had the opportunity to sail on the Irish Sea. Our boat was a traditional Manx fishing boat of a style popular 100 years ago. It was a 20-some-foot replica built for a documentary film. The mast was about 18 feet long, a sturdy ash pole, tapered at the top and less than 5 inches in width where it went through the forward seat. The sail was less than 100 square feet, and was almost square. It was sewn from sturdy cotton canvas sailcloth. It had reef points so you could make the sail smaller if the wind increased, and it had been dyed a reddish brown color to replicate the linseed oil and ocher mix that was painted on the linen sails of the nineteenth century to protect the fabric.

At first I thought the boat would be underpowered with such a small sail, because most of my experience had been sailing one-design racing boats designed for relative low winds less than 15 miles per hour on inland lakes and rivers. As we rowed out of the harbor, the wind grew in strength until it was blowing twenty miles per hour and more. We hoisted the canvas sail and then we were off. The old fishing boat shouldered its way through the chop and soon we found ourselves making pretty good time out to the entrance buoy of the main channel. We sailed out to an island about an hour away for lunch and then returned to the harbor for a pint at the local pub. The little sail was adequate for the job.

In comparison, I have a racing sailboat about the same length with an overall weight of 850 pounds, and a 30-foot mast carrying approximately 300 square feet of sail. This is a fun and safe boat in a ten-mile-per-hour wind; in fifteen miles per hour the boat is a handful, and in a stronger wind you need to reduce sail area and head for the harbor. In the fishing boat replica when we encountered heavy gusts, the mast just gave a little and the small sail shrugged off the wind at the top like it was designed to do. The owner told me later that the boat weighed 1,600 pounds and could carry 1,000 pounds of fish in the hold. He had once taken the boat out with friends and returned with the wind blowing almost thirty miles per hour. They felt quite safe with a reefed sail. I thought about my boat, and in those conditions I would probably have capsized. You can always go conservative on sail size, and add more sail for light air days, and reduce the area for windy ones. The skiffs we are building are designed for sheltered water. However, watermen did occasionally find themselves caught out when weather took a turn for the worse. They made do the best they could; the simple boats often did better than the fancy ones when the going got rough.

Daggerboard and box

A daggerboard provides lateral resistance, allowing the boat to sail upwind. Another similar method uses a centerboard, also referred to as a center plate. The daggerboard slips into a daggerboard box and can be pulled completely out. The box is fastened to the bottom of the boat and sits over a slot cut into the bottom for the board to slip through. The centerboard box also fits over a slot in the bottom of the boat. A centerboard works on a pivot and the board is retained in the box. Usually the top of the box is fastened to the front of the rowing seat for support and is well above the waterline. This prevents water from coming into the boat.

There is a lot of science involved to determine the exact shape of daggerboards and centerboards, and their placement in the boat. We want the board to provide resistance and be positioned in the optimum center of effort of the sail. This can really get confusing. I do what the old skiff builders did: Put the slot and box in front of the rowing seat and use the rowing seat for support, and everything will work fine.

You want the box to be slightly larger than the daggerboard that slips into it. Sometimes the board will swell a bit, so having a minimum of ½-inch all around the board is best. Then you will never have a problem with the board binding in the box.

The science of creating a performance daggerboard involves creating the optimum foil shape, much like an aircraft wing. These boats are not performance sailboats, so a simple board to provide lateral resistance is easy to make. A sailboat 12 to 15 feet long can use the same size daggerboard; however, the bigger boat would be better with a daggerboard about 10 inches longer. I make my daggerboards from ¾-inch marine plywood or two ½-inch panels glued together if I want a board one inch thick. The laminated thicker board works well for a larger boat. Most of my boards are 10 to 14 inches wide and 40 inches long. You can experiment with these dimensions and settle on a size you like the best. An inch or two here or there will not make much difference with these skiffs. Round the leading edge and taper the trailing edge for the best water flow around both edges. I typically use a large dinner plate to draw a curve on the leading and trailing edge bottom corners. You can leave the bottom of the daggerboard square, too.

I usually build my daggerboard boxes from laminated ½-inch marine plywood, so I have a box that is a full one inch on each side. If I am building a very small skiff of about 10 feet in length, I will use ½-inch ply for each side. One-inch sides would be overkill for such a small skiff. To make it easy, I use common 2×4s for each end. The plywood is then glued and nailed to the 2×4s, making a very strong box. I always try to give the inside of the box a heavy coat of paint before assembly. Sometimes I forget, though. You can always do it later with a narrow foam roller, if you wish. There can be a lot of stress on the box when it is windy, so I always fasten the boxes firmly to the middle seat. I use a common galvanized angle iron as a front brace that is screwed into the daggerboard box and into the boat's bottom and anchored into the rub strip. If you are going to make your skiff into a sailboat, always add a bottom rub strip and skeg.

To install the daggerboard box, place it over the inside bottom of the skiff in front of the rowing seat. Use a long pencil, or tape one to a stick, and trace the inside dimension onto the boat bottom and draw your slot. Cut the slot and make sure the box sits evenly over it. Sand it smooth. If you used ½-inch ply, you will need to increase the bottom width by gluing ply or another wood to the sides of the box to provide more material for the screws. This material need only be about 3 inches up from the bottom of the boat. Use plenty of bedding compound here. Screw the box down tight from the outside, coming up into the box framing. Make sure to attach the rear of the daggerboard box to the middle rowing seat and the 90 degree angle iron in front. This will keep the assembly rigid. Sometimes I make the box with a notch in the back, so the notch will just slip under the seat. I then place two long screws through the seat into the box to keep it in place.

I use the daggerboard method for the simple boats I build, because they are much easier to construct and less complex than centerboards. Centerboard pivots have a tendency to leak, because they are usually under the waterline. There are methods for building the pivot above the waterline, but the complexity increases. If the centerboard is wood, it may float up and not stay below the boat. Therefore, a wood centerboard would need to be weighted with lead or iron. Many times, a metal centerboard is used so it will sink, hence the term center plate. If your daggerboard floats up, make a small wedge to keep it in place.

Rudder

Many rudder styles will work for these skiffs. Some fishing skiffs would use one oar for a steering sweep, and the other oar as a mast. This is the ultimate in simplicity and it works pretty well once you get used to it. A purpose-built rudder will work the best, though. A rudder for skiffs of this type should have two-thirds of its surface area under water to be effective. Make a simple rudder and experiment with it. The bigger boat will use a larger rudder.

Fashion the rudder the same way as the daggerboard. You can use marine ply or laminated planks. Treat the leading and trailing edges the same as the daggerboard. Play around with the design and make it look pretty. Try them out on your model.

There are many methods of attaching a rudder to the transom. Today most rudders are attached using a hinge assembly made of a socket and pin. The socket is called a gudgeon, and the pin, a pintle. On historical replicas I have seen everything from rope and leather attachments to wood gudgeons and iron pintles greased with tallow. All methods seem to work just fine. You can purchase this hardware from marine suppliers referenced in the resources section of this book. I like to experiment, though, and have found that galvanized farm gate hardware found in most hardware stores works well.

Tillers

A tiller is attached to the top of the rudder and allows the rudder to be controlled so you can steer the boat. On skiffs the tiller is a simple affair, usually 3 feet or so in length. Even though the tiller is nothing more than a steering stick, it can be decorated to give the skiff a distinctive look. I like to add a few curves whenever possible. A slightly curved tiller, with a carved round end to the hand grip and wrapped with cord, can enhance a simple tiller. A few curves added to the rudder also improve the visual effect. I have often used replacement tool handles for tillers. They are easy to use and made from good quality hardwood. Cut them down to fit your application. A pretty rudder and tiller attached to a raked transom takes the simple skiff to another level.

Spars

Spars support the sail. They can be the simplest affair, like an oar, or more complex. When I was a kid, I made a mast from an old closet rod and a sail from a bed sheet. I steered the boat with an oar. The summer wind came from the southwest, and I had a straight run upstream about a mile from our house. Wind follows the path of least resistance, so as the breeze funneled into the main body of the water, I was carried up to the next bend of the river, where I would turn around and row and drift back to our dock. Later I wanted more performance, so I made a proper set of spars, a real rudder, a daggerboard, and a better sail from an old painter's tarp.

For these skiffs simple solid wood spars are a good choice. A mast 10 to 12 feet long works well and can be stored in the boat. These masts will be free-standing; the sail area will be small enough that support rigging is not required. Spar wood has traditionally been lightweight, straight-grained spruce. This wood is not easy to find at your local lumber store, but can be ordered from specialty suppliers. The downside is that it is expensive.

For a short mast of 10 to 12 feet, you can laminate 2×4s or 1×4s and then shape them with a hand plane or spoke shave. For the boom and top spar for a simple lug rig, use a 2-inch fir closet rod or a shaped 2×2. All of the spar connections can be made from rope. I know this sounds really simple, but these sail arrangements were often made from discarded oars and broken spars from larger boats. Nothing was wasted. I was given a nice 12-foot wooden boom from an older one-design racing boat, and I still use it as a mast for my 12-foot

skiff. Look around at a marina or a sailing club. Often this stuff can be had for few dollars or for free.

For boats like we are building, the sails were lashed to the spars with small-diameter rope. Modern synthetic rope looks out of place on these boats, even though it is vastly superior to the natural products. Use what you can find. I buy manila rope from the hardware store and coat it with pine tar and a little beeswax and let it dry in the sun. After a few days I rub the rope down with an old pair of leather gloves and work in the beeswax. The beeswax stiffens the rope and gives the fibers a "good hand." This provides some water resistance and UV protection, too.

Running rigging to manage the sail should be as simple as you can make it with a pulley or two (called blocks in the maritime trade) and a cleat on the seat or gunwale. You want everything to be wrapped around the spars so the sailing rig can be stowed out of the way in the boat when not in use. Blocks purchased from marine suppliers are built to withstand the heavy dynamics of racing boats. A simple single block to handle a ⅜-inch line can cost $50 or more. These are precision-machined items. You can use hardware-store pulleys for a few dollars each on our boat.

I once had a huge collection of blocks and other marine fittings scavenged from boats

that were headed to the junk pile. Over the years I have used them all up on various projects or given them away to desperate sailors needing a part or two. You can always look around at a boating club or marina and see what you can find. Another alternative is to make your own stuff. I fashion all of my cleats now from hardwood soaked in linseed oil and pine tar, and they work great. For my skiffs I rarely use blocks any more. I make simple thimbles made from oak or other hardwood, cut them out, and shape them with a wood rasp and sandpaper. I drill a big hole in the middle of the thimble and smooth it with a round file and sandpaper. For example, with a ⅜-inch manila line you should have a ¾-inch hole. Greased up with tallow or beeswax, your line will pass through just fine. For hundreds of years these worked well. Little boats got what worked and nothing else.

Here is a tip about locating small hardwood pieces. Find a custom cabinet shop in your area and ask them what they do with their cut-off waste. By doing this, I usually walk away with a big box of oak, hickory, walnut, cherry, and other fine woods. It will likely be free if you tell them what you are going to do with the wood. Woodworkers and craft folks like to help each other out.

Cats, Cat Rigs, and New England-style Catboats

This design variation is a bit different from the flatiron skiff; however, it follows the basic principles we have already discussed, and is a nice alternative if you wish to go this direction. The type of boat we are talking about is not the twin-hulled beach catamaran with brightly colored rainbow sails seen at many resorts. These are fun boats and are often just called "cats" by catamaran sailors, but this is not what we will be building.

All boats with a single sail, whether twin or single hull, can be called a cat-rigged boat, and no one really knows the origin of the term. A single sail is enough to power many small boats safely, and a moderate-size sail is the best choice for the flatiron skiff designs

The New England-style catboat originated in the middle of the nineteenth century in the Cape Cod region primarily for fishing in shallow waters. These sailing boats are very wide. For example, an 18-foot catboat might be up to 9 feet wide. They carried a short, stubby mast up front and a large sail, which could be reduced to a smaller size as the wind increased. They had large centerboards and huge, shallow-draft rudders to correct for the severe-weather helm caused by the big sail up front. With the sail up front in the bow, the boat wants to turn with the wind, and a big rudder can force it back on course. These big rudders are referred to as "barn door rudders," which means that it took a rudder the size of a barn door to steer them.

Thimbles example rigged on my catboat.

These boats have a tremendous cargo capacity, can operate in very shallow water, and are fast. In the late nineteenth and early twentieth centuries, these boats were often fixed up for the weekend crowd for an excursion on the bay. A 20-foot catboat could easily seat ten paying guests and two crew members.

The hulls on these boats were usually rounded, and sometimes flat bottomed, with the rounded bottom creating more volume and able to hold a larger catch. There are many styles and sizes of these boats, which are still popular today. They are an interesting-looking boat with their wide beam, one line to manage the single sail, and your other hand on the tiller.

I have an 11-foot catboat with a 5-foot beam. I built it a long time ago from plans designed by Charles Whitholz. It is his version of a small dinghy catboat with a canoe-type bow and a barn door rudder. This boat has a rounded hull design. A friend of mine started it and gave it to me, and I finished it with help from my father. I will pass it on to my children some day. It has a personal value. I call it *Little Jonah*.

I have built several round and flat-bottomed versions of these boats. I like them because they have a wide beam and are easy to set up and fun to sail. I also think they look pretty good, because I always get a lot of attention when I pull up to the dock. The flat-bottomed version is the one we will discuss, because it is easier to build than the rounded-bottom one. This version is built similar to the other skiffs, with a few minor changes to accommodate the wide beam.

Use all plywood for the wide-beam hull. It will be easier to bend than solid planks. Make your planks about 12 inches wide and scarf them as before. Instead of 12-foot planks, 14-foot planks or longer will better allow for the wide beam. If you scarf two 8-foot plywood panels end to end, you will have a 16-foot plank. This should be sufficient for a 14-foot catboat.

When building a flat-bottomed catboat skiff, I use a 60-inch spreader stick. This will ensure a nice, wide hull. The transom width should be 48 inches at the top. I like to put a little more twist in the lower planks; to do this, measure in 3 inches on each side at the bottom of the 48-inch plywood transom panel. Measure as before and remove the leftover material. Save it for later use, and brace the transom with 2×4s just like the other boats.

I also prefer a little more transom rake. This is arbitrary, but it gives the flat-bottomed catboat a sleeker look when sailing. However, most of the old round-bottomed catboats from the nineteenth century had plumb transoms. So you can do what you wish. Once again, make a model and then decide.

Lay out your bottom plywood planks. Use a minimum length of 14 feet to allow for the wide beam. As I said, most of the time I make 16-foot planks from the plywood and see how everything looks before cutting them to a shorter length, and if you do this your overall boat length will be in the neighborhood of 14 feet. Make transom-locating cleats as before.

Example of a lug rig sail with a boom. A boom stiffens the bottom of the sail to maintain its proper shape; ideal for light winds. Even though this sail is on a round bottom catboat it will work just as well on a flatiron skiff.

Use the same type of spreader stick and soup can arrangement.

You could use the same daggerboard as you would use on the sailboat, but for catboats I like them a little wider: 16 inches is fine, and at least 36 inches of the board should be under water. Laminate two ½-inch ply panels together to make a 1-inch-thick daggerboard. Build your box strong and anchor it well. A 16-inch-wide board will have more stress on it than a narrower board. Always leave extra room in your daggerboard box to prevent jamming.

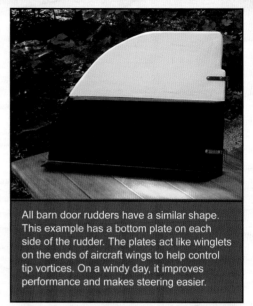

All barn door rudders have a similar shape. This example has a bottom plate on each side of the rudder. The plates act like winglets on the ends of aircraft wings to help control tip vortices. On a windy day, it improves performance and makes steering easier.

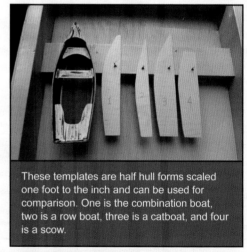

These templates are half hull forms scaled one foot to the inch and can be used for comparison. One is the combination boat, two is a row boat, three is a catboat, and four is a scow.

The barn door rudder is very simple. It is approximately a quarter circle in design and is fitted to a raked transom in one of two ways. You can cut the angle on the rudder to match the transom angle, or you can use a trimmed filler piece that matches the transom angle but

Boat shed and author at work.

sets the rudder in a vertical position. I have used both and I prefer the vertical arrangement; I believe it provides better rudder control. When I do this I also anchor the filler piece into the skeg. Feel free to experiment.

The catboat bottom will require three or more sheets of ½-inch plywood. The thicker plywood adds more stiffness to the hull, and you will need two additional bottom braces— one in the front and one toward the rear. The rest of the boat is built the same as the other examples. You can use the same size sail as on the other skiffs, but I prefer a slightly larger sail on the catboat, because the wide beam needs the extra power to drive it. A 100-square-foot sail is more than adequate.

Example of a lug rig sail on my catboat. Note the absence of a lower boom. None is required on these small sail rigs. There is nothing to hit you in the head when tacking.

Scow Skiffs

A scow is a flat-bottomed boat with a blunt bow. The name scow comes from the Dutch work *schouwe*. These boats were first developed in Europe to carry large bulk loads in shallow water. The boats were very large and many were over 100 feet long. In the nineteenth century, scows could be seen sailing on all coasts of the United States. They were cheap to build and could be sailed by small crews. Popular on large bays and the Gulf Coast, they were considered the heavy haulers of work boats.

Even though boxy-looking, these boats were fast, and refined versions of them are still raced today. Before the age of racing catamarans, they were the fastest sailing boats in the world; some were clocked at almost thirty miles per hour.

In its simplest form, the common john boat is a type of scow. They sometimes go by other names such as a garvey or a punt. I like scow skiffs, because they are very simple to build with a transom on both ends. The bow transom is usually smaller than the stern transom, but it doesn't have to be. The boats can be slab-sided or have the flare of added volume. All versions perform well. The main drawback is that some people find them unattractive. One fellow told me that the boat I was building was nothing more than a box 16 feet long by 4 feet wide with three seats. I agreed with him, but added, "This box won't sink, and I'm going fishing tomorrow and haven't spent $100 to build it."

The little scow sailboat I like the best is built just like the New England catboat, but instead of messing with the stem, build another transom for the front similar to the one in back. Put a little deck on the front to support the mast. A 12-foot scow skiff 5 feet wide can easily support four people with a small cooler and a picnic for an afternoon sail, and if you build it four feet wide it will fit in the back of a full-size pickup truck with the tailgate down.

Materials

Look in the back of any boating magazine that caters to wooden boats and small craft and you will find an endless list of suppliers for wood, adhesives, fasteners, hardware, specialty tools, sails, and other items. These are good sources. I have a library of books dedicated to boat building and nautical lore. Many of these books were first published 100 years ago. The information in them is interesting; however, much is no longer relevant and usable. A good example is the use of white and red lead for boat building. Those items are still around, but as I said previously, I no longer use them. There are many modern equivalents, some are better than the items they replaced and some aren't. You still can't beat pure tallow for dressing your oar leathers, and it soothes your hands, too, after a day of rowing. It takes some research to locate items like this, but they can be found. (See resources.)

Wood

The choices of wood to use on the boat can be very confusing. The skiffs in this book have probably been built with every type of wood species imaginable. Some of the expensive marine plywood and solid wood come from African and South American forests that are being decimated at an alarming rate. I always check my wood species and and will not support suppliers that do not follow sustainable practices. Sadly there are many bogus products out there, too, especially when buying plywood. Years ago, when most plywood sold in this country was made here, quality wasn't an issue. Inspect the products closely. Many are now being made in Asia, Africa, and other locations around the globe. Much of it is falsely stamped by the manufacturers to bring higher market prices. True marine plywood must bear an official stamp; it is made without any voids in the inner plys, and waterproof glues are used throughout. Most of these waterproof glues are dark in color. If the plywood has a very light glue color and is marked waterproof, check with your lumber supplier and ask to see the data sheets from their vendors.

With plywood, I sometimes do my own testing. I cut up 4-inch squares of wood and boil them in a bucket outside on a camp stove for about an hour, and then leave them out in the weather to see if the plys delaminate. I do this outside because often the wood really smells when I boil it. I had some wood once that smelled just like a pig farm. I don't know what the glue was made from, but the wood plys came apart in about ten minutes and left a strange residue in my bucket.

Not all bargain wood is bad; I am often pleasantly surprised when I test it. For example, I have made inexpensive skiffs with underlayment plywood. In order to be certified underlayment, the plywood must have no voids and be made with waterproof glue. It is half the price of marine ply and is good for testing a design idea. If you choose to use bargain wood, know the risk. Sometimes everything works out, and sometimes it doesn't. Get to know your wood products. Your labor cost is the same using poor or good-quality materials.

This brings up an often asked question: Why not just buy marine plywood? My answer is this: If this is your first boat and you only want to invest a minimum amount, follow the instructions in chapter 2. Use the best ¾-inch exterior grade plywood you can find in the stack for your transom. Only a small portion of it will be in the water. Make the upper planks from the best ⅜-inch exterior grade plywood you can find. These upper planks will be well above the waterline. Seal all the exposed plywood edges well with paint, varnish, or wood oil. Spend your money on the next boat project.

Fasteners

I am continually trying out different fasteners and other related products, too. For several years now I have been using the twisted, hot-dipped galvanized deck nails for some applications. They are hard to remove. I use them in places where I need extra holding power and a screw is not practical. I am often asked why I don't just use screws all of the time. I do use screws where I think they are needed and no other fastener will work. I don't use an electric screw gun much, and even though my "Yankee" screwdrivers work well, placing a thousand or more screws is hard on the hands.

Why not just use a battery-powered screw gun? Well, those batteries are getting better, but when they die, the replacements are very expensive. I have a five-gallon bucket full of dead batteries I need to recycle. I think I'll continue as I have been doing.

Another thing about screw guns: Most folks use battery-operated drills that both bore holes and install screws into the wood. These are fine products; I have several and I do use them on many projects. Most of them now are variable speed. It takes some adjustment on the builder's part to learn how to drive screws at slow speeds. Most of the woods we use for these skiffs are soft woods like pine and cedar. Even though tulip poplar and sassafras are considered hardwood, they are not as dense as oak, ash, and maple. With a modern power driver it is easy to split the wood and even shear a screw. Without careful attention, the screw is driven so fast that you lose control. Many of the modern screw fasteners are bugle heads. These are designed to be self-countersinking in some materials; however, when driving them fast they often split soft woods like pine and cedar and lock up in hardwoods, breaking the screw. With handpowered screwdrivers, it is very difficult to split a plank. You can tell if the plank is going to split before it happens, and you can back out the screw and deal with it. The "Yankee" type screwdrivers, also called automatic drivers, are still available at woodworking stores. Not all are the same quality, and you get what you pay for. The best are made in Germany and England.

Square, hex, and star drive screws are much superior to the older-style slotted screws. They provide a positive connection between the fastener and tool bit. Designed primarily for powered screw guns, they also work well for the hand screwdrivers, reducing "slip-out" that can damage the wood surface.

Slotted screws still have their place, though. With a proper driver that fits correctly in the slot, these screws can perform well. Although designed in the nineteenth century, Phillip, or hex, screws were later chosen for auto industry assembly-line production. They were easy to drive with air-powered tools but would "cam out" before being over tightened. Most do-it-yourself woodworkers do not own the specific sizes of slotted screwdrivers to match various-size slotted screws. And many of the screwdrivers available now are poor quality—the steel alloys are inferior and may not be heat treated correctly. I have a set of Marples cabinet-grade screwdrivers that are about seventy-five years old, and I will not give them up.

Sadly, most of the slotted screws being machined today are not consistent from batch to batch. Unless I am building to a historical period and want a certain look, I don't use the slotted screws. When I do use them, I purchase quality bronze screws from a marine supplier. They are expensive, but they outlast the cheaper products.

In the days before epoxy glues, boat builders would often have a tub of grease or tallow for lubricating screws and nails. The grease made the job easier and prolonged the life of the fastener. The grease and tallow didn't hurt the wood, and all of the finishes were oil-based anyway.

If I am building a big skiff and need to use 3-inch or longer nails, I stick them in grease. If you are going to drive nails like this into oak frames, you will need to drill pilot holes for the nails. Even then, it is best to grease the nails. A little grease can do wonders for many things on a wood boat. On sailboats I make sure everything that moves or comes in contact with the weather is well lubricated, even the rigging screws that tension the shrouds. I know this sounds old school, but it works for me. Tallow—rendered beef and other animal fats—works well on traditional rigging and boat parts. Prepared properly, it will not turn rancid and has little smell.

Epoxy doesn't stick very well to greasy spots, and two-part polyurethane coatings don't like it, either. If you're using epoxy, you need to make sure everything is very clean before application. I remember washing down surfaces with acetone or MEK (methyl ethyl ketone, also called Butanone*), before applying expoxy. These organic solvents are water soluble and have the ability to dry out a surface quickly before it is coated, improving adhesion. However, when used on the skin to remove epoxy and paint, these solvents rapidly remove moisture and oils. Because they are water soluble, they can enter the bloodstream through the skin and cause all kinds of organ damage. Nice stuff! That is another reason I no longer use epoxy and related products.

1. What is this boat going to cost?

The magic number is $500 or less. The secret is controlling waste, using standardized fasteners, and avoiding expensive epoxy and other coatings that aren't appropriate, anyway, on traditional-style wood boats.

I have several old books with great boat designs. The costs in these books reflect the time in which they were published. If you encounter a situation like this, take the book's materials list to a lumber store and price everything out. Once you have an idea what things will cost, look the design over and see where you can trim costs, or find another design if you are on a tight budget. You may discover that after researching various designs, a simple 12-foot or 14-foot boat may work just fine for your needs. A good used outboard motor may cost as much as the materials, and a sailboat will cost more than a rowboat. You can always build the less expensive boat first.

Frequently Asked Questions

2. How long will it take to build?

The first-time builder should allow 100 labor hours or more to complete any configuration of the flatiron skiffs discussed in this book. Unless you have created a deadline for yourself, what's the hurry?

This brings up a story with a sad ending. Several years ago I was asked if I wanted to purchase an uncompleted forty-foot cabin cruiser. The fellow started it when he was a young man and had dreams of building the boat and taking it down the Mississippi River after his retirement; he planned to eventually travel across the Gulf and live in Florida. This was his dream and not his wife's, nor the rest of the family's. In fact, the wife had grown to hate the boat and everything about it. He had spent thousands of dollars, countless labor hours, and he was still not finished when I was called.

Now he was older and in failing health. His life-long dream would never be completed. He wanted me to tell him what the boat was worth so he could sell it. This was hard for me, because I don't like to bring bad news to anyone. The two engines he had purchased many years ago would not run well on modern unleaded and alcohol supplemented fuel. Some of the wood on the hull was beginning to rot, too. The list went on, and I finally told him that selling an unfinished project of any kind would be difficult. I could see the disappointment on his face. Later that year he paid to have the boat hauled off.

I see this situation frequently. Go to marinas and boat yards, and there are always abandoned projects stuck in back lots with weeds and small trees growing around them. The good news is that when you build your skiff, you can finish it within a reasonable amount of time. You will not have spent a fortune on materials, and you can usually sell it for what you have in it. Even if you end up giving it away, you have had fun and learned a thing or two.

3. What is this concept of building without plans?

Let's look at it this way: In the past, when trades were learned through apprenticeships and over a period of years, by the time you were told by the yard foreman to go out and build a 16-foot boat, you had learned enough to just go and do it. Plans weren't required, because the steps were etched into your brain by the long, arduous time spent working with a master of the trade. None of us has ever learned anything overnight unless it was a very simple, repetitive task. This is why in the first part of the book I suggest starting out on a few simple projects to hone your skills.

Building by eye is similar to playing improvisational music. There is always a structure or design architecture that you work within. When building by eye and without plans the basic structure is there. Perhaps it exists in a photograph or a sketch or in the builder's mind. What I like about building this way is that it allows me to push myself further and be more creative. I don't do crazy things like building a 6-foot-tall cabin on a 12-foot boat. If I did, the proportions would be all wrong and it would be unstable. So then, how do you know when you have exceeded design limitations? The easiest way is to keep the basic skiff form in mind all of the time, make subtle changes at first, and if those work, make a few more changes on the next build. As you improve in your skills

push yourself to try new things. Remember you can always experiment with models, discard or keeping those ideas as you go.

When I was a child, an interesting couple lived a few houses up-river from us. Tom and Polly had immigrated from Ireland and came to Chicago about 1910. He had worked as a floor carpenter laying wood block floors in factories until his retirement after WWII. They moved south to our neighborhood about 1950. I was about six years old when I first met them. Our school bus would stop in front of their house, and on winter mornings they would let us stand in their kitchen and wait for the bus. They never had children of their own, so we were special to them; they gave us fresh, hot treats to take to school.

To supplement their meager retirement income, Tom caught fish from the river and sold them in the neighborhood, and Polly taught piano lessons. You could always go to their house and get fresh fish, and when their garden was producing you could also pick up vegetables. Tom was the local fix-it guy, too. He would fix outboard motors, lawn mowers, coffee pots, tin pans, and just about anything else. He also built nice little boats he called "cots."

Years later I came across several of these boats when working in Ireland. They are flat-bottomed, not unlike our skiffs, and used on

local rivers for catching salmon. He told me that he had learned to build them from his father. As Tom grew older, his vision worsened and it became difficult for him to continue boat building. Toward the end of his life I remember helping him bend the planks into position and drive the nails. By then, he could barely see unless it was a bright day. He would run his hands along the planks and tell me to plane a little off here and there before setting the next one. Tom never used plans. The designs were in his memory and his memory went to his touch. He could feel when something was not correct. Being a kid, I was always in a hurry to get to the next step, and Tom would tell me that Mr. Hurry would make a mess of things if you let him, and that he built boats simple and plain, because simple was easy and plain lasted longer than fancy. I do my best to follow his advice today.

The basic skills of building by eye can be picked up quickly; the rest is an accumulation of knowledge gleaned through study, observation, and trial and error.

4. How do I know what paint or finish to use? There are so many choices.

Paint chemistry has changed a great deal, even in the last few years. Several factors have pushed the science along. One of the biggest is the demand for coatings to adhere well and stand up to harsh environments over time. Painting anything is costly, and consumers want good value. The other factor involves a better understanding of lead and its dangers to humans and the environment. Along with this, we now have more knowledge of VOCs (volatile organic compounds) and the role they play in air quality.

In days when paint primarily covered wood, linseed oil-based paint would soak into the wood, carrying with it pigment, lead, some of the turpentine, and the drying chemistry that contained metals. Most of the turpentine would evaporate, leaving the paint film. These paints also contained a material called whiting, which is finely ground chalk. If you rubbed your hands over the dried paint film, it would leave a dusting on your hands. As the paint aged and the linseed oil broke down, the chalky surface became more prominent. There were enamels available that would not chalk off so quickly, but when these aged they had a tendency to chip off in flakes and blisters. So you had two choices—either paint every year or not paint at all; or paint maybe a little color stripe for an accent. Most of the wooden work skiffs weren't painted until paint technology improved.

Good paints are available that replicate the best qualities of the older style but contain no lead and are fast drying and easy to clean up. (See resources.) They are not cheap, because these are specialty coatings designed for the salt-laden marine environment. Fewer wooden boats are in use today, so the paints are not formulated in large quantities. This contributes to higher costs, too.

I started experimenting with acrylic paints several years ago for surfaces above the waterline. In general, I am pleased with the results. They do not have the gloss retention of oil-based paint, but I don't want a high-gloss finish. It shows all of your imperfections, such as areas where you forgot to sand. Occasionally, I will use gloss paint for a stripe, on areas I want to highlight for contrast, or on a small piece of trim. I also use varnish in limited amounts.

All paints formulated for exterior use contain UV (ultraviolet light) inhibitors. For clear coatings to withstand the marine environment, they must contain the maximum amount of UV inhibitors. Clear coatings include non-pigmented oils, varnishes, and waxes, as well as a few non-varnish substitutes. When UV inhibitors are added, most of these coatings take on an amber appearance as the layers increase. Professional painters who do a lot of marine varnishing say that at least six coats, sanded between each coat with 600-grit or higher paper, is the minimum standard for a good job.

Light, semi-gloss colors work well because they hide imperfections better than dark colors. Trim always looks good as a contrast, whether it is painted darker, stained, varnished, or oiled. In the resources I have included a source for "Down East" linseed oil and pine tar finish. It smells like an old boat yard out of Lord Nelson's Navy and is about as traditional as it gets. I have read that many of the traditional wood boats that plied the historic monsoon trade routes between the Middle East and China were coated with a mixture of sheep and goat fat, with animal hair worked into the seams. Take your pick.

5. How do I bend the wood for the side planks?

Virtually all wood today is kiln-processed. A common kiln-dried 1×12-inch pine or cedar plank will likely conform to the degree of bend we require. You can also use the weather-bending technique described in chapter 2.

A shorter boat may require a narrower beam in order for the planks to bend easily. However, you can make a 12-foot boat with 16-foot side planks—longer planks bend more easily than short ones—and cut off the extra. For example, you would attach the soup can hinge as before, measure back from the front about 5 feet, and place the spreader stick. Then bend the two planks into position and attach the transom. After this is completed, cut off the remaining wood and use it for seats, a deck, braces, and so forth.

The wood will tell you when it has reached its bending limit. It will become more difficult to bend as you approach its failure point. Sometimes you can hear the wood fibers as they are compressed on the inside of the curve and elongated on the outside. Many times I grab both planks, squeeze them toward one another, and close my eyes to help me better feel the tension in the wood fibers. I have done this so many times now that I can tell when planks are about to break. Another technique is to bend the planks slowly and repeatedly until you reach the desired bend.

If you want to experiment, bend two planks to failure. You can use the broken pieces for seats. You will be surprised by how much pressure it takes to break a 1×12 16-foot plank. But each plank is different. I have been able to bend some planks into a double-ender—a skiff with two pointed ends. Most of the time, though, you will not be able to do that with lumber from the average home improvement store.

The standard finished size now for 1×12-inch lumber is ¾-inch thick and 11 inches wide. Because I no longer have a shop with a lot of power tools, if I want a thinner plank I must take my boards to a mill and have them planed to the desired thickness. Some lumber suppliers catering to professional contractors will do it for a nominal charge.

If you want to build a skiff with lighterweight planks, I suggest using three or four planks to a side instead of two. You can use 8-inch instead of 12-inch planks. Narrower planks will bend easier than thicker ones; properly braced, they can be made strong. The choice of wood is important, too. Cedar wood is lightweight and strong and can be milled quite thin and still be serviceable, but some cedar species are brittle. Atlantic white cedar is a good traditional boat-building wood and is still available at a reasonable cost. Keep in mind that the skiffs we are going to build were usually made from local wood. Use what you can find easily.

6. What bottom planking options can I use if I don't want to use plywood?

Before plywood, the only option was to use solid planks. Flat-bottomed skiffs were usually cross planked. This is a technique where short planks are fastened and caulked next to each other across left and right chines. Think of chines on a flat-bottomed boat as the bottom edge of the lower plank. On other types of boats, it can mean something else. The short planks are strong and do not need extra bracing. For a 16-foot boat, you would need bracing every foot or so if the bottom planking was placed fore and aft. Both methods are acceptable. Bottoms planked with boards and not plywood should be caulked correctly to make them tight. They also need to soak in the water so that the wood swells, making the joints tighter and leak-proof.

Most boats planked in this fashion will leak some, and years ago, no one worried about a few leaks. They all leaked a bit. As the hot sun baked the bottom of the boat during the day, a few seams would open up slightly and water would work its way in. If an inch or so of water was kept in the bottom of the boat, the planks would not shrink in the sun as much. At least that was the theory. These planked boats were kept in the water during the boating season to keep the planks swollen and tight. If you cross-plank a skiff hull correctly, it should tighten within a day or two after launching. The problem comes about when the boat is kept on a trailer most of the time. The planks dry out, and sooner or later gaps form between the planks.

This condition can be prevented by cross planking with spline joints and using waterproof glue on the splines. The bottom can also be double planked with muslin between the planks soaked in waterproof glue. Essentially, you are making composite bottom similar to plywood. When leak-proof fiberglass boats came on the scene it is easy to understand why frustrated boat owners sold or gave away their leaky old wood boats and bought fiberglass ones.

When cross planking a boat, you can get a tighter bottom by using full-dimension one-inch lumber, because you have more surface area to accept your caulking and it makes a stiff bottom. To get this planking dimension today, you must have it milled or plane it yourself from thicker stock. For skiffs of the sizes we are building, common 1×6 cedar or pine lumber is adequate. Small, tight knots are okay, too. Rough-cut your planks to size, leaving about two inches extra, and lay them out on your upside-down boat. Make sure you have made your hull planks square to the cross planks. You don't want any light showing under the planks. Next, number the planks with a pencil from front to back so the order can be repeated. Also at this time, draw a pencil line

under the planks next to the boat hull. Remove the planks and plane a slight angle on each edge, so that when they are placed back on the boat there is a little V-shaped groove between each plank. This groove will provide room for your cotton string and bedding compound. Also, cut a saw blade thickness on the outside of the mark you just drew around your boat to remove excess wood. At this point, it is easy to follow the slight angle and curve on each plank with your saw. If done on the boat, it can be very difficult with a handsaw because of the hull flare. Some builders make this trim cut with a power router after they have fastened the planks.

Next, carefully spread bedding compound on the hull plank edges all around the boat. Get a ball of cotton string, and, starting at the front of the boat, push the string into the bedding compound right in the middle of the hull plank edge, going all around and coming back to the front. Do this as neatly as possible. Bedding compound dries slowly, so you will have plenty of time.

I like to begin cross-planking from the center of the boat out to the ends so that if I need to trim off wood or add a piece, I can do it without tearing everything off and starting over. If you preplanned your planks and numbered them beforehand, everything should work out. However, it is wise to have a way out of a bad situation if you need it. When cross-planking, I like to get someone to help me at least with the longer middle planks. Lay the planks down into the bedding compound and try to not disturb the string position. Push them next to each other and fasten them down with one nail in the middle of each cross plank. Depending on the wood quality, you may need

to drill pilot holes for your nails. After the planks are down, add more fasteners—total of three for each 1×6 inch plank. If you choose to use narrower cross-plank material, use a total of two nails per plank. Check over your work and add the required fasteners to do the job. When cross-planking, I prefer to use hot-dipped, galvanized twisted nails. These grip well and will not pull out as the planks swell in the water.

After you have completed these steps, the grooves between the cross planks must be primed with an oil-base wood primer. You can prime with thinned oil-base paint, like the old-timers did. Next, press your cotton string down into the cracks between the cross planks. You don't need to use anything special like caulking irons for these skiff bottoms as you would on a larger boat. I have a dull putty knife I keep around for jobs like these. If the crack is large, put in a few extra pieces of string. On bigger boats you would use caulking cotton, but string is fine for these boats. Let the string hang out about 4 inches from each crack as you work around the boat, then pull it downward and snip it off. Do this all around the boat. Now spread your bedding compound into the cracks on top of the string, working the compound into these seams. Once the compound has skinned over, you can paint the bottom of your boat. Start out with thinned oil-base paint and let it soak into the wood. Come back in a few hours and add three more coats of paint, waiting about four hours between coats, or follow the manufacturer's instructions.

There is another method of cross-planking. It is crude by some standards; however, I have seen this done all over the world, so it must have some merit. You also need to use 1-inch or thicker planks; anything less will tend to buckle once water-soaked. Prepare your chines as before and position the cross planks, numbering them so they can be reinstalled in order. Instead of making a slight angle on the edge of the planks for caulking, plane them so they will lay tightly next to each other and cut them to fit. Instead of bedding compound, use pine tar or roofing tar spread on the bottom edges. You will not use any string. Next, lay your planks into this mix and immediately begin to nail the cross planks down, forcing them tight together with galvanized twist nails. If the planks are 1 inch thick, you will need 3-inch nails. When the bottom is planked mop hot tar over everything. You may need several coats of tar; let the coating dry in the hot sun. Using the tar method, it is easier to tear the whole bottom off if you choose to go back to a painted bottom. This method works best for large, heavy working skiffs over 18 feet long.

Many of today's wood boats eliminate bottom leaks by encapsulating the wood with epoxy resin and cloth. This can work, but sometimes it doesn't. I build both cross-planked and plywood-planked bottoms, and I don't use epoxy. I make the tightest bottoms that I can, I paint the bottoms with at least four coats of oil-based paint, with the first coat thinned enough to soak into the wood. If there is a little seepage, I throw a sponge into the boat and go fishing anyway. The world is not perfect, and I accept that.

7. What stem options can I use?

There are many options, some easier than others. A traditional stem can be cut from a solid piece of lumber that is large enough to include all of the dimensions. For example, a stem for a 16-foot skiff can be carved from a solid piece of 4×4 fencepost lumber. You would use a rule and angle gauge to lay out the design and then cut it with sharp chisels, a wood rasp, and then perhaps a plane, and finally sandpaper. If you had access to a band saw and table saw you could use those tools, but much of it will still require hand work.

You can build an I-beam stem with three 2×4s glued and fastened to look like steel beam. You can make a T shape with two 2×4s. These stems will give you about a 12-degree angle on both sides for a total of about 24 degrees. They are good for long, narrow rowing boats. You can use a single 2×4 with the side planks toe-nailed into it. These were pretty popular when a 2×4 was a full dimension. Not so much now with today's finished lumber.

My favorite is the soup can method, which is explained in chapter 2. Using this method, the correct angle is determined when the side planks are bent into shape. Then all you need to do is cut the stem wood to the required angle. The cutting can be done on a band saw, table saw, +, or split with a hatchet and cleaned up with a plane, or use a plane for all of the shaping. In the northern latitudes in Scandinavia, parts of Russia, and countries around the Baltic Sea, an ax, hatchet, adz, draw knife, saw, and plane are virtually all that is used to shape the stem, transom, and planks. Sometimes I like to split out the stem wood with a hatchet if I have good, straight-grained wood. These are good skills to learn. Many of the wood boats built today use a complex multi-piece stem arrangement. These are fine for some boats, but for simple skiffs I prefer the easiest choice: a single 2×4 or 4×4 shaped to fit.

8. Can I build these skiffs using only plywood?

Yes, plywood will make a nice boat. Use the 4×8 sheets of plywood panels as your lumber source and cut your wood planks from the ply. I like to cut the plywood into planks and then use these as I would use any other wood. If you want a narrow plank, cut it accordingly. Your planks will only be 8 feet long, so you will need to join them to make them longer. This is called scarfing. There are several scarfing methods that use tapered ratios. This can get complicated. The easy method is to make a butt block from wood to hold the two panels together, as explained in chapter 2. Many builders today use epoxy and cloth instead of wood blocks. The two plywood panels are joined together with epoxy resin, and then fiberglass tape is placed on each side and soaked with epoxy resin. Wax paper is placed under the joint to prevent the panels from adhering to the work table. When everything cures, in about 24 hours, you can sand the joint smooth on both sides. This is a common method, and the now 16-foot panel will bend pretty well

and you can use it just like a standard wood plank. For our skiffs, ⅜-inch marine plywood is sufficient for plank material.

I use a traditional wood block butt joint. Most of the time I make my blocks from ¾-inch marine plywood, glued and screwed into place with PVA glue. The wood butt blocks only go on the inside and are out of sight. You can make these blocks from solid wood, but the grain must be rotated across from the plank grain to prevent them from splitting.

Most plywood boats built today are saturated with epoxy resin and covered with one or more layers of fiberglass cloth and more resin. This makes a very strong, water-resistant hull. If you have a large plywood boat, it is probably better to spend the extra effort and cost to glass your boat. Your paint finish and wood will hold up longer.

You don't have to do this, but be aware that paint alone does not hold up very well on some wood species made into plywood. Thin plywood veneers will begin to check and destroy the

paint finish. Checking is caused when the veneers contract and expand, and hundreds of tiny little cracks form along the grain. Coating plywood with epoxy and cloth prevents checking. Douglas fir marine plywood is very strong and a good value, but it checks more than the other species made into plywood.

I paint my plywood skiffs and deal with the checking by giving them a light sanding in the spring and repainting them. It only takes about a quart of paint to cover a 16-foot hull above the waterline. I usually use acrylic paint for topsides now, because it dries quickly and the repainting each year is less of a chore. If I paint my boats at all, I most likely will use light green paint, and one or two gallons will cover a lot of boats. It is much less expensive than epoxy resin and fiberglass cloth, and it isn't toxic. The traditional green color is a reminder of the boats I grew up with.

9. Can I use epoxy, and what does "stitch and glue" mean?

You can substitute epoxy glue where I have used PVA glue. Plywood in itself is a composite structure made from thin veneers glued together under immense pressure. Plywood is dimensionally stable and works well with epoxy resin, fiberglass tape, and cloth. Many of the

kit boats use an assembly method referred to as "stitch and glue." The marine plywood panels are cut with CNC (computer numerical control) software that contains the coordinates for the patterns. The panels are then fastened together using plastic zip ties, copper wire, and even

common tape in some applications. This part of the process is the "stitch." Once the panels are assembled, you have a boat shape. Fiberglass tape and epoxy is used to bond the panels and make it rigid, hence the "glue" part of the process. After one side is complete, the ties or wire are removed and the other side is fiberglassed and glued. To make the seams even and stronger, a thickened epoxy resin is spread into the joints. This thickened material can be purchased or made by adding various materials to the epoxy to give it a thick viscosity like creamy peanut butter. A great deal of sanding is required to even out rough spots and blemishes. This process produces a lot of toxic fiberglass and resin dust. My primary reason for not using epoxy is that I am allergic to it after years of sanding the resin. Anyone sanding epoxy should wear a filtration mask. For those who develop an allergic reaction, it often causes problems on bare skin, too. I would need to suit up with special coveralls.

10. When I go to the home center there are many kinds of caulking available in the paint section. Can I use these?

The short answer is no. True marine caulking is designed to perform in a constantly wet and salty environment. Most of these caulking products are not cheap; they are messy and require a variety of solvents to remove them from you as well as unwanted areas of your boat. They are made from polyurethane and polysulfide and other similar products.

There was a time when caulking meant the act of caulking, the complete process of priming, hammering in the cotton, filling the seam with a compound and then painting to ensure a watertight seal. This definition is still true; however, if you walk into a store and ask for caulking they will direct you to an aisle where many different tubes of caulking compound are on display. If it is a marine store most likely they will be of the marine type mentioned. If it is your home store they will primarily be products for filling cracks and minor holes on your house prior to painting. Most of these will be acrylic latex products designed to work well with acrylic paints. If you read the labels closely, all of these will state they are not suitable for marine use or below the waterline. If the home center is in a maritime region they may carry marine grade caulking. If the label doesn't say for marine use it is not for marine use.

The skiffs made a hundred years ago never had a bit of polyurethane, polysulfide, or silicone caulking in them. These products had not yet been invented. So what did they use? Most of the products came in a can, not a caulking tube. They were formulated from a variety of ingredients such as white lead, linseed oil, and pine tar, milled cotton for filler, ground chalk, and metallic driers. Some worked pretty well and others not so good. All of the boats that used these products were made from wood. When fiberglass boats came on the scene these older products did not stick well to the resin and glass composites; therefore, new formulations were developed that would work. Within the last sixty years these marine caulks and sealants have been improved to provide good service in harsh environments.

As an inexpensive alternative above the waterline, use acrylic paints for the topsides of your skiff, then purchase the better quality acrylic caulking tubes at your home store, and cover it well with paint. If you are going to use an oil finish on your topsides above the water line you can use common rope caulk from the hardware store or regular painter's oil based putty. Rope caulk is very user friendly. It comes in a package that is scored so you can peel off small strips, knead it in your hands and press it into areas where you need to fill. Rope caulk and putty are usually gray, so if you need a dark wood color just mix in some walnut stain. Like bedding compound it never really dries much and you can dig it out years later if you need to. I have used this material below the waterline; but I don't advise it, because below the waterline compounds like Dolfinite are readily available.

11. Why have two masts and two sails on a small boat? Won't one work?

Yes, one will work fine; however, two masts—one in front and one in back—have certain advantages. In a strong wind, two 50-square-foot sails are easier to work than one twice as large. Two shorter masts also make the skiff less top-heavy in windy conditions. Many of these boats were worked in winter. With a boat rigged with two sails the foresail could be lowered and stowed out of the way and a bow anchor lowered over the side. Leaving the aft sail up, the boat would weather cock with the bow toward the wind and ride comfortably while the waterman worked the traps or fished. After the catch was completed, the foresail could be raised once again for the trip home. If the wind had increased even more, the sailor could lower the aft sail and concentrate on sailing back to port with only one smaller sail in front. These different combinations of masts and sails were all designed as working rigs to make life on the water a little easier and safer.

The Skiff Builder's Art

Mastering any trade takes study and practice. By the time you feel confident in your abilities, you look back and discover that you have spent a lifetime at it. It does not matter if your medium is wood or something else. Few people have a personal understanding of the time and effort it takes to build something well, because so few of us need to build things anymore, unlike the old-timers. Here are a few things I consider important in this endeavor.

A can-do attitude

In America during the first half of the twentieth century, many endured hardship, financial upheaval, war, and other obstacles. Those who made it through were strengthened by those events. They were not afraid to do things that they might not be totally familiar with. I grew up watching people fix and build things without special training. Some of the stuff they built might have looked amateurish, but most of it was functional. Therefore, give yourself a chance. Start slow, build up your skills, and then build your boat.

I also believe that anyone who has ever built a water craft and then taken it out on the water must have a streak of independence. In my classes, I like to see a certain amount of independent thought mixed with a desire to help others learn a new skill.

Understand your limitations

Few of us know our limitations because we are rarely pushed to exceed them. In boat-building, you quickly figure out the point where you need to ask for help or do more research. This is why I like future builders to start out on small projects and work up to the big ones. Your limitations are exceeded each time you learn something new.

Basic knowledge of tools and how to use them

A hundred years ago, most schools had manual arts training. This training covered many skilled trades that no longer exist today. We now have a generation with little understanding of how things are made and maintained.

There are fewer repair shops now, and our current culture of disposability reduces the need for the skills to support these crafts. This is changing, though, as schools are reviewing the importance of the manual arts and applications training. With the popularity of do-it-yourself entertainment and educational programming, stores in every region of the country provide materials, how-to workshops, and advice. Take advantage of them.

Make time

People have always been busy, but our priorities are different now than in the past. For example, when I teach my skiff building classes, I do my best to find a venue close to my students, and I hold classes on Saturday mornings from nine until noon for about six weeks. That is as much time away as people can take from their normal activities.

How do you make time? Try turning off the television, get up earlier in the morning, or stay up longer in the evening. Use more of your personal time off. Treat your boat building as a priority and make it a personal time for yourself.

The most creative people I know have a day packed with activities. One friend works on her art projects into the night, sometimes after her family has gone to sleep. To her, art is an essential part of her life. She explained that without it, she would not be a whole person. When I worked as an engineer for a large jet engine manufacturer, I researched wood boats during my off time and practiced sketching so I could replicate the interesting boats I saw on trips. I took our children to the library, museums, historical sites, and a lot of walks on docks all over the country.

Even on small boat projects, I work out a building schedule and do my best to keep to it. I love little boats because people can usually fit these projects into their busy lives.

Enjoy the process

I had a student who couldn't relax. Everything he did had to meet his rigid sense of perfection. It took a lot of effort to get this fellow to lighten up and enjoy the class. We made a few mistakes on that skiff, because we were trying some new things. In the end it sailed well enough to get the family who rented it back to the dock after their propeller was damaged on a rock ledge.

I tell my students there is plenty of time to choose that one boat design that requires flawless perfection and execution, and until that time, have fun along the way.

Final Thoughts

I became interested in boats when I was about ten years old. Growing up on the river and watching boats go by was fascinating to me. I couldn't get enough. I also grew up around old craftsmen who had a clear understanding of what it meant to build by hand and eye. These were generally quiet men, and few had time for a kid hanging around. So I had to watch, and then ask good questions. I also had to listen closely; they talked in hushed voices and mumbled, a tendency no doubt acquired when talking on the job was discouraged.

A few of the guys did take an interest in my curiosity, like my neighbor Tom, my two uncles, and my father. My father was a machinist who was good with tools and math, had impeccable handwriting, and could spell more words than most. In his twenties he built a fishing boat from plans he bought for a dollar at the local lumber yard. I can still remember fishing in that old boat with him. We caught a few fish, of course, but most of the time was spent in discussion and discovery.

When my father was in his eighties he started clipping pictures from boat magazines and building scale models. The first were basic, but he improved as time went on. We continued discussing the skiff builder's art long after his old fishing boat rotted away at the lake cottage. I now have about twenty of his models; many are museum quality. He was ninety when he started the last one, and I helped him finish it about a year before he passed on to where old boat builders go to sail through eternity.

I refer to my tiny shop as the boat shed. There is a clear running creek below my house that flows into Northern Virginia's Potomac River a short distance away. With the rivers and the Chesapeake Bay nearby, there is a long history of boat building, beginning with the settlers of Jamestown. I grew up in Midwest corn country; unless you were on the Great Lakes or the big rivers, working boats were scarce.

Here it is different. To this day, there is a seriousness about the working boats and the watermen who ply their trade. Each time I build a skiff, I am reminded of them. For me, skiff-building isn't just about hammering planks together. It is about trying to get a better understanding of the culture and history of those who make their living on the water.

In the days of working sail, to meet the requirements of an able-bodied seaman you had to hand, reef and steer.

Being an "able hand" meant you had an understanding of rope, rigging, sailor's knots, sewing and keeping the sails in good order, rowing and working as a team, ship carpentry, and maintenance.

Being able to "reef" meant you had the knowledge and courage to climb up the mast into the rigging and manage the sails with your mates and take the sails in (reef) or shake them out (full). Reefing was tough physical work and not for the faint-hearted. A hundred feet up or more on a swaying mast and yard arm, you were expected to use one hand for yourself and one for the ship.

"Steering" meant following a course on the compass and keeping the sailing master's heading, by not only watching the compass but watching the sails, feeling the movement of the ship and understanding what it meant, and keeping an eye on the weather and reporting any changing conditions to the officer on watch. The job of steering a ship was left to the most competent crew members. The tiller man had everyone's life in his hands.

After years at sea, many of these sailors made their way into the boat shops along the coasts, Great Lakes, and navigable rivers. The watercraft they built reflected their knowledge and skills. As times changed, so did the technology, and fewer and fewer sailors made their way into these crafts. Today, there is little need for a wooden ship fitter, ship carpenter, traditional rigger, barrel maker, caulker, or ship blacksmith. However, each time you build one of these flatiron skiffs by hand and by eye, you are carrying on an honorable tradition. Go build your boat.

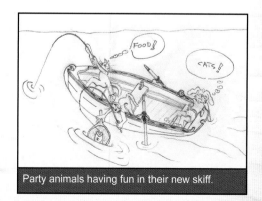

Party animals having fun in their new skiff.

Appendix

The following companies and resources can provide everything required to build a boat. This is not a complete list, just a few sources to get you started. I suggest an Internet search for local suppliers. I have had a positive experience with all of these companies.

American Rope & Tar. They offer genuine Stockholm tar and other traditional wooden boat products. 8115 River Front, Fair Oaks, CA 95628, tel. 877-965-1800, www.tarsmell.com.

Atlantic Sail Traders, Used sails. 1818 Mango Avenue, Sarasota, FL 34234, tel. 800-946-3800, www.usedsails.com.

Bacon Sails & Marine Supplies. Used and new sails. Annapolis, MD, www.baconsails.com.

Boulter Plywood. Marine plywood of all types, marine lumber, milling services, long lengths, and nationwide delivery. tel. 888-4BOULTER, www.boulterplywood.com.

Defender. Marine outfitter since 1938. 42 Great Neck Road, Waterford, CT 06385, tel. 800-628-8225, www.defender.com.

Hamilton Marine. Traditional marine hardware and supplies, for boat builders, sailors, fishermen, and commercial operators. 155 E Main St., Searsport, ME 04974, tel. 800-639-2715, www.hamiltonmarine.com

James Town Distributers. They supply a wide variety of boating materials from hardware to fasteners, adhesives, paint, books, and product advice. 17 Peckham Drive, Bristol, RI 02809, tel. 800-497-0010, www.jamestowndistributors.com.

Marine paint for wood boats. Traditional oil-based products are made in limited runs and you will not find them at DIY stores. Different brands can be ordered from the marine suppliers listed. Ask for color chips.

Marshall's Cove Brand Marine Paints. Traditional high solids alkyd-based enamel made with high-quality resins for marine environments. PO Box 10244, Bainbridge Island, WA 98110, www.marshalls,covemarinepaint.com.

George Kirby Jr. Paint Company. Makers of marine paint for over 150 years. New Bedford Massachusetts, www.kirbypaint.com.com.

Noah's Marine, Marine plywood, tel. 800-524-7517, www.noahsmarine.com

PolySail International. Low-cost sails from white poly tarp material, kits and instructions. 2291 SE Gaslight St., Port St. Lucie, FL 34952, www.polysail.com.

Shaw & Tenney. Oar and paddle makers since 1858, they carry rowing and other related products and tallow lubricant, oar length formulas, and oar placement information. PO Box 23, 20 Water Street, Orona, Maine 04473, tel. 800-240-4867, www.shawandtenney.com.

Traditional Boat Supplies. A British company with items no one else has, right out the nineteenth century. They ship to the US and will walk you through the steps for US Customs. 31 Ravensmere, Beccles, Suffolk, NR34 9DX, tel. +44(0)1502-712311, www.tradboats.com.

West Marine. They supply a wide variety of boating materials from hardware to fasteners, adhesives, paint, books, and product advice. 500 Westridge Dr., Watsonville, CA 95076, www.westmarine.com.

Woodcraft. More than seventy locally owned stores nationwide supply tools, wood, finishes, books, tool sharpening services, and advice for the woodworker. Search the Internet for a store near you.

Bibliography

Beston, Henry. *The Outermost House*. New York, NY: Holt, Rinehart and Winston, 1985.

Buehler, George. *Buehler's Backyard Boatbuilding*. Camden, ME: International Marine, 1991.

Chapelle, Howard, I. *American Small Sailing Craft*. New York, NY: W. W. Norton & Company, 1951.

Chapelle, Howard, I. *Boatbuilding a Complete Handbook of Wooden Boat Construction*. New York, NY: W. W. Norton & Company, 1941.

Gardner, John. *Building Classic Small Craft Volume 1*. Camden, ME: International Marine Publishing Company, 1984.

Gerr, Dave. *The Nature of Boats*. Camden, ME: International Marine, 1995.

Greenhill, Basel. *Archaeology of the Boat*. Middletown, CT: Wesleyan University Press, 1976.

Kemp, Peter. *The Oxford Companion to Ships and the Sea*. Oxford, UK: Oxford University Press, 1988.

Leather, John. *Clinker Boatbuilding*. London, UK: William Collins Sons & Company. Ltd, 1987.

Monk, Edwin. *How to Build Wooden Boats with 16 Small-Boat Designs*. New York, NY: Dover Publications, 1992.

Monk, Edwin. *Modern Boat Building*. New York, NY: Charles Scribner's Sons, 1949.

Payson, Harold. *Build the New Instant Boats*. Camden, ME: International Marine Publishing Company, 1984.

Pilkington, Roger. *Small Boat in Southern France*. New York, NY: St Martin's Press, 1965.

Rössel, Greg. *The Boat Builder's Apprentice*. Camden, ME: International Marine / McGraw-Hill, 2007.

Smith, Harvey, G. *Boat Carpentry*. New York, NY: Van Nostrand Reinhold Company, 1955.

Steward, Robert, M. *Boatbuilding Manual*. Camden, ME: International Marine Publishing Company, 1970.

Thoreau, Henry, D. *Walden and Other Writings*. New York, NY: Modern Library, 1992.

Verney, Michael. Complete Amateur Boat Building. New York, NY: The Macmillan Company, 1948.

Witt, Glen L. *Boat Building with Plywood*. Bellflower, CA: Glen L. Marine Designs, 1967.